Pure Patriotism

by Clayton Thibodeau

Dedication

This book is dedicated to all those who protect and defend the Constitution of the United States of America. I humbly extend my thanks and sincere gratitude to them and to my family and friends who inspire me and give me hope and courage.

About The Author

CLAYTON D. THIBODEAU is an American. He is also a construction technologies professional and an educator; holding an MBA and an MAED (Master of Arts in Education) from the University of Phoenix. Clayton has been happily married to Lori Elizabeth Williamson for 22 years, and they have been blessed with two daughters, Christina Marie and Ashley René. Though he has lived most of his adult life in Southern California, Clayton has also lived in Texas, Utah, and upstate New York. Clay enjoys fishing, philosophy and film, but mostly, he enjoys freedom. Basically, Clayton D. Thibodeau is an American Patriot: a real, live, Red-White and Blue-to-the-bone citizen of the Greatest Nation ever conceived in the history of humankind.

You are invited to visit Clayton Thibodeau on the web at:

www.clay4usa.org

CONTENTS

Issues of Our Generation

Duties and Mantra

Pure Patriotism

Patriotism is generically defined as the love of and devotion to one's country. With this accepted, how does one measure his or her own patriotism? Perhaps it can be measured by what one feels or believes, or by exploring why one does what he or she does? After all, our motivations and intentions are, if nothing else, a measure of our thoughts and feelings and beliefs – from which our love and devotion spring.

While it is true that intensions are important and meaningful, what is done has much more impact than the reasons why – what we do always outshines our motivations.

This book is not about just any form of patriotism, it is about American Patriotism: it is about love, respect, devotion, and allegiance to the Constitution of the United States of America and to the Country and People it protects. This book is about what patriots must do, and despite the appearance of contradiction with the previous paragraph, this book is about why patriots must do it.

As you read Pure Patriotism, please consider the following thoughts on what Pure Patriots care about and what they do not:

Patriots do not care where you choose to live; they care that you are safe in your home. Patriots are not preoccupied with how much money you make or how you earn it; they are concerned about your freedom to choose your own education and career paths. Patriots are not obsessed about the color of your skin, your sexual preferences, or your political affiliations; they are devoted to your right to choose for yourself what you will believe, and say, and do. If patriots have a singular obsession, it is to the preservation of the Constitution of the United States of America and to liberty and to equality for all.

Purpose

"A patriot" is something that you are, the question you must ask yourself is: to what are you a patriot?

"Patriotism" is something that you live: it is what you believe, and say and do. Exposed within your thoughts, and words and actions are the keys to unlocking your patriotism: they are the signs that reveal the nature and character of what you love and where your true devotion rests.

This book, like your patriotism, is a work in progress, how could it be otherwise? Patriotism isn't done yet!

Together with the publication of this book, I, the author, am launching a website: it is here that our conversation will continue and where the gathering of American patriots is welcome. Because the issues facing American Patriots are ever changing, how could one possibly hope to answer the cause of pure patriotism in a single writing? So please, visit me and your fellow American patriots, we are waiting for you at:

www.purepatriotism.com

If you are able, while reading this book, have your copies of the Constitution of the United States of America and the Declaration of Independence handy, these documents will be extensively referenced.

First Edition

Clayton D. Thibodeau

www.clay4usa.org

www.purepatriotism.com

ISBN 978-0-578-02536-0

Founding Documents and Patriotic Psalms

Excerpt One from the Declaration of Independence
July 4th of 1776, Preamble

"We hold these truths to be self-evident, that all men are created equal, that they are endowed by their Creator with certain unalienable Rights, that among these are Life, Liberty and the pursuit of Happiness – That to secure these rights, Governments are instituted among Men, deriving their just powers from the consent of the governed."

Beautifully written and barely comprehended in our generation. So, what were these enemies of the Crown and patriots of the American Colonies saying to the world and speaking to us: their posterity?

These earliest of American patriots sought to explain that they did not agree with one another on the origins of humankind. Some believed that the God of the Christian's was the Creator, while others believed in God, but not the God of organized religion. Still others of the American Revolution believed in Science over religion or that the natural evolution of man was their Creator. But in unity, they could agree that regardless the title, they did not create themselves, and as such could state undeniably that humanity was made of a "Creator."

As we all share a common unity in creation, regardless what form the Creator, that common unity makes of us equally endowed with those rights that are not to be alienated, or removed, or taken, or suppressed from us. Our brave Founders specifically identified three rights given universally to each of us, and these are: the right to life, the right to liberty, and the right to pursue happiness.

The preamble concludes with the most foreign declaration of the time: that the power to govern is endowed within the people. That not by force of arms or by royal bloodlines does a government acquire its authority to govern the people, but rather, by the free consent of the people themselves – and further, that the singular purpose of the government is to protect and defend its people's rights to life, liberty and the pursuit of happiness.

Imagine the boldness of such a declaration. Today we may take such a claim for granted, but in 1776 such a declaration by the fledgling offspring of England would have been something indeed: commoners of European decent claiming equality with the kings and emperors of the world.

And more still, these Colonials state unequivocally that the role of governments is to serve their people. Consider how this might be received in a country like Japan, where the people believed that they were governed by their "Creator."

Today, some 230 years later, we Americans still debate the origin of humankind. But sadly, we no longer stand united in our acceptance that we are equal inheritors in the endowment from our Creator. We would rather argue and battle over the origin of our creation, than respect one another's views.

I say to you here and now, for so long as we defend our own beliefs about creation, and do all possible to assault the institutions and symbols and beliefs of those with whom we differ, we can not claim in honesty that we are American patriots. For that which most distinguishes an American patriot is the characteristic of fighting for and defending the lives, the liberties, the happiness, and yes, the beliefs of those with whom we do not agree.

Excerpt Two from the Declaration of Independence
July 4th of 1776

"Prudence, indeed, will dictate that Governments long established should not be changed for light and transient causes; and accordingly all experience hath shewn, that mankind are more disposed to suffer, while evils are sufferable, than to right themselves by abolishing the forms to which they are accustomed. But when a long train of abuses and usurpations, pursuing invariably the same Object evinces a design to reduce them under absolute Despotism, it is their right, it is their duty, to throw off such Government, and to provide new Guards for their future security – Such has been the patient suffering of these Colonies."

Few more meaningful and profoundly applicable statements could be uttered today, with respect to our own governance. Regardless your political leanings, you must rightly agree that our political leadership has been utterly corrupted by their unquenchable thirst for power.

Unlike the then inhabitance of the thirteen Colonies, the Americans of today do not suffer despotism at the hands of a distant king. Nor do we suffer evils under the formation of a tyrannical domestic government – rather, we are the willing suffers of suppression and harassment by our own, duly elected "professional politicians."

Patriots must stand posts in political offices if we are to take our country back from the professional politicians, and restore our Constitution to its place of honor and dignity.

Excerpt Three from the Declaration of Independence
July 4th of 1776

"He has erected a multitude of New Offices, and sent hither swarms of Officers to harass our people, and eat out their substance."

In context, the "he" referred to in this declaration was the then King of England. Today the "he" more rightly describes the professional politician. Nevertheless, the balance of this declaration has never been more applicable in the "New World" of the Americas, than it is today. Our politicians have established offices and swarms of officers to regulate and harass our people for all manner of private and personal activity. As for the "eating out of their substance," this primarily refers to taxation and the seizure of personal property. Consider this partial list of taxes and harassments:

They police and tax the light bulbs in your table lamps; they police and tax the electricity that illuminates your light bulbs; they police and tax your food and your beverages, your job and your employer; they police and tax your income; your vacations, your retirement; your vehicles; your fuel; your music; your movies; your shopping; your heath care; your inheritance; your telephone calls; your television watching; your driving; your parking; your smoking; your gambling; your investing; your land; your education; your sidewalks; your streets; your guns; your ammunition; your homes; your social security; your bank accounts; your heaters; and your coolers –

If you can imagine it, you can be certain there is a federal politician out there who has devised a way to police and tax it; and if not, there is another federal politician out there who is desperately trying to find a way to do so.

To illustrate this point, let's talk for a moment about your favorite babysitter. For the purposes of this illustration, let's say that your babysitter is a 16 year old girl, and that you pay her $25 per night to watch your children.

According to the Internal Revenue Service (IRS), and brought to you directly from your friendly politicians in Washington D.C., if you hire your babysitter twice a month, you must by law report her to the IRS for taxation. Even though she will not likely owe income tax, there are other taxes the IRS does want to extract from your babysitter. For starters there is the Social Security Tax and the Medicare Tax, but the list does go on. Because you have paid her more than $599 in a single calendar year, you are expected to complete a 1099 form on your babysitter: with her name, address, Social Security Number, and the total amount you paid her for the year – and deliver that 1099 to the IRS for processing. If you fail to do so, you will be liable for her tax withholding along with some hefty fines and interest penalties to boot.

Now, before you go telling me that I am being ridiculous because nobody actually files 1099's on their babysitters, and car washers, and housekeepers, and yard maintainers, and such; please keep in mind that just because nobody does it, does not mean that it is not the law of the land. This flawed thinking is no more-true than the idea that because everybody does a thing, it must be legal. Try telling that to any one of the millions of citizens who pay speeding tickets each year for driving 5 miles an hour over the speed limit.

Truth is, when the IRS comes-calling, there is nothing to prevent them from throwing the book at you: extracting taxes, and fees, and penalties, and interest, and the entire ball of wax. Your government taxes every dollar you make when you earn it, and they fully intend to tax it again when you spend it.

If you think you live in the same "free" America established by those who wrote the Declaration of Independence, after dumping all that tea in Boston Harbor back in 1773, it is only because your liberty has been stolen from you so progressively that you do not know the difference.

At this moment, federal politicians are seizing private businesses from thousands of your American neighbors, without due process and without compensation, and placing those businesses under foreign ownership and control.

The patriot recognizes that professional politicians have high-jacked our Government and usurped our Constitution. But the patriot loves this Country and the Constitution as earnestly as the family and friends that bring meaning and purpose to life. The patriot waits eagerly for enough citizens to recognize what is obvious: we patriots need to unite and vote-in "new Guards for our future security!"

I would that able patriots stood willing to take posts as "guardians" in government offices, rather than suffering in silent despotism. We do not need bullets, we need ballot votes; and we do not need militia soldiers, we need "citizen politicians."

Excerpt Four from the Declaration of Independence
July 4th of 1776

"For taking away our Charters, abolishing our most valuable Laws, and altering fundamentally the Forms of our Governments. (Colonies/States)"

The professional politicians of Washington D.C. have for several generations progressively and systematically invaded our States and our communities, to transfer power and authority from "we the people" to the Federal Government: this, to feed the never satisfied appetite for power that is the Central Government – together with the professional politicians who hold post therein.

And while millions of American citizens have been beguiled by the promises and allure of a large and powerful Central Government, the patriot recognizes that power corrupts and that even well-meaning politicians can not long endure the serpent.

No, my dear friends, a large Central Government has but a singular objective, and that objective is to feed and grow fat on the substance of its citizens. To grow is its one design and its one obsession.

The patriot looks honestly and objectively at the landscape of America and is brought to tears at the knowledge that we stand at the very precipice of falling. The patriot stands proud as an American, and ashamed to have allowed the professional politicians to bring this Great Nation to the brink of desolation, to the edge of that final stroke that will erase all memory of liberty and freedom.

Excerpt Five from the Declaration of Independence
July 4th of 1776

"He has excited domestic insurrections among us."

Without possible debate, it is clear and obvious to even the most passive of observers that the politicians of our age have attained their respective positions of power as the deliberate and purposeful result of exciting citizens to argument and to aggressive posturing one against another. Our politicians have very effectively segregated our population of citizens into dozens of factions (special interest groups); mustered those factions into opposing political parties (Democrats and Republicans – predominantly); and then pitted our citizenry against itself.

By illuminating and elevating our social differences, rather than that which unites us, professional politicians have accomplished what the King of England could not – they have divided and conquered us: they have subjugated us to our own Government and then entrenched themselves within its positions of authority.

The patriot recognizes in near dismay that the brother his father loved, and the sister her mother cherished, have become enemies at each other's gates. We must unite as a people and care for and celebrate one another for our differences and uniqueness, or we will be utterly enslaved to our elected politicians by the hatred and domestic insurrections they excite among us.

Excerpt Six from the Declaration of Independence
July 4th of 1776

"A Prince whose character is thus marked by every act which may define a Tyrant, is unfit to be the ruler of a free people."

We must vote the current politicians out of offices of authority and replace them, by election, with citizens devoted to the Constitution and to liberty – and not to a thirst for power.

Excerpt One from the Constitution of the United States of America
September 17th of 1787, Preamble

"We the people of the United States, in Order to form a more perfect Union, establish Justice, insure domestic Tranquility, provide for the common defense, promote the general Welfare, and secure the Blessings of Liberty to ourselves and our Posterity, do ordain and establish this Constitution for the United States of America."

More beautiful words have rarely been spoken. Not we the Congress; not we the Senate; not we the representatives; not we the politicians; but rather, we the "people!" And it is this patriot's opinion, that it is high time we the people took back the Halls of our Government, by the constitutionally prescribed method – the VOTE!

We would be better served today by political leaders selected from the citizenry by lottery, than we have been by the last several generations of Democrat and Republican politicians – between which we have been compelled to choose. Voting for the lesser of two evils is still voting for evil! If the Democrats and the Republicans can not find patriots from among their ranks, it is time to form a more perfect Union without their contributions to the political system. Because the candidates of the more recent quarter century have dismantled our Justice system; have incited domestic Insurrections among us; have weakened our national defenses; have favored individual Welfare over general Welfare; and have at every possible opportunity robbed us of the Blessings of Liberty enjoyed by our Forbearers – they stand unworthy of continued service.

For clarity's sake, allow me to digress into a brief definition of the phrase "general welfare," which digression I take because I so frequently hear this phrase misinterpreted and miss-applied to the social and human conditions of our generation.

Specific Welfare is individual Welfare; ie: Welfare reserved for a single individual or group or class. General Welfare, in contrast, is Welfare available to and accessible by all citizens: equally. Thus, general Welfare refers to Welfare which is equally distributed among all citizens: Welfare that does not favor or disfavor one individual or group or class over another individual or group or class.

The reason this phrase found its way into the preamble of our Constitution is because it was vitally important to the Founders, and to their Posterity (us), and to the preservation of the Union (the United States of America) that our Central Government not engage in selective or discriminatory practices; ie: practices that would benefit one citizen or group or class to a greater or lesser degree than another citizen or group or class.

You will note the continual application of this theme throughout the history of American governance. Not until February 3rd of 1913, with the ratification of the 16th Amendment to the Constitution, had the Federal Government enforced significant central control over the lives, and liberties, and pursuits of individual citizens. From that date hence, however, the Central Government has progressively and exponentially expanded and increased its involvement in and its control over the citizenry of the United States of America.

Pure American Patriotism demands that we the people re-ordain the Constitution of the United States of America by voting for "Citizen Politicians" who vow to restore the Constitution as the Federal Rule of Law.

Excerpt Two from the Constitution of the United States of America
September 17th of 1787, Article 1, Section 2

"Direct Taxes shall be apportioned among the States according to their respective Number of Persons. The actual Enumeration shall be made every subsequent Term of ten Years, in such Manner as they (Congress) shall by Law direct."

September 17th of 1787, Article 1, Section 8

"The Congress shall have the Power To lay and collect Taxes, Duties, Imposts and Excises, to pay the Debts and provide for the common Defense and general Welfare of the United States; but All Duties, Imposts and Excises shall be uniform throughout the United States."

September 17th of 1787, Article 1, Section 9

"No Capitation, or other direct, Tax shall be laid, unless in Proportion to the Census or enumeration herein before directed to be taken."

These three sections of Article One of the Constitution represent the totality of the Taxing Powers granted the Federal Government by the people of the Unites States. There is a singular characteristic of these Taxing Authorities that is clear, distinct, and unavoidable: citizens are not to be singled-out as individuals or as groups for the purpose of Taxation.

Consider this, there are two types of Taxes which the Central Government is empowered to impose: (1) commerce taxes, and (2) direct taxes. Commerce taxes are taxes upon the sale or trade of goods and services. Direct taxes are taxes upon people.

Expressly noted in Article One of the Constitution are these limitations: (1) "Commerce Taxes shall be uniform throughout the United

States," and (2) "Direct Taxes shall be apportioned among the States according to their respective Number of Persons."

Of particular interest to the patriot is that the Federal Government had no authority to:

1. Tax the citizens of the United States by any method or measure other than by their apportioned number of persons, which tax was excised (collected) from the respective States and not directly from the citizenry, or

2. Name or otherwise identify or classify the individual citizens of the United States, or

3. Lay commerce taxes within or upon the activities of one State in greater or lesser proportion to that of another State.

By all measures of interpretation, it was the intent of the Constitution to limit the grasp of the National Government by limiting Government's vision to these overriding imperatives: All States are Equal in the Eyes of the Federal Government – AND – All Citizens are Equal in the Eyes of the Federal Government!

Patriots recognize that this does not describe the Federal Government of the present century. Something has changed and that change has limited the Life, Liberty and pursuit of Happiness of our citizenry.

And though patriots have been up and down this road dozens of times over the decades, following the ratification of the 16th Amendment in February of 1913, it is important to understand how this could happen when the language of the Constitution is so clear and so explicit in its meaning and purpose and design. So let us look now and consider the words of the 16th Amendment to the Constitution:

"The Congress shall have the power to lay and collect taxes on incomes, from whatever source derived, without apportionment among the several States, and without regard to any census or enumeration."

The vary tenor of the language is itself tyrannical: "from whatever," "without apportionment," and "without regard."

The 16th Amendment to the Constitution of the Unites States of America perfectly and precisely executed our fate as surely as with a guillotine. With one stroke and one singular sentence, our elected representatives mocked us and our Constitution. Turning their backs on 126 years of American sacrifice and history and our constitutionally protected way of life, the three branches of our Central Government (Executive, Legislative, and Judicial) colluded and did seize mastery over us.

Have you begun to see and consider it? In this one stroke of conspiracy between the three branches, they (professional politicians and Judges seated in perpetuity) penetrated State's rights and pierced the heart of we the people. We were made serfs to our own government and the freedom we had enjoyed and the liberty we had cherished was confounded. Let us enumerate the undeniable and the undisputed:

1. Our federal politicians gave themselves the authority to tax individual citizens, without the protection of the States, and without the restriction of apportionment – meaning they could tax each individual citizen by differing measurements and by different discriminatory standards, and

2. Our federal politicians gave themselves the authority to name, number, and otherwise identify and classify individual citizens by any manner or methodology they choose, and

3. Our federal politicians gave themselves the authority to alter the standards of taxation from State to State, and from activity to activity, and from citizen to citizen in accordance with their own discretion and for their own purposes and designs.

In 1913 the professional politicians of the United States of America, duly elected by the people and with the willing blessing of the Supreme Court, created the first identifiable "class" in our free nation: they made of themselves the "Royalty" of America.

To disguise their conspiracy, they created enmity between the rich and the poor and the so-called middle class — "classes" which did not previously exist. That is right — prior to 1913 we were equal citizens in the "eyes of our Government." In a country where the poor could become rich in a matter of months or years, the poor looked upon the rich as the potential of what they could achieve and become. And those in the "middle" represented the American Dream — they represented what average effort and average ingenuity could grant to an American citizen.

Prior to 1913 persons of other nations would migrate to the United States for either of two predominate reasons: (1) to escape oppression and enjoy individual freedom, or (2) for the opportunity to acquire personal wealth equal too or greater than the average American. Because compared to the opportunities elsewhere, the standard of living of the average American far exceeded that of the other nations of the world.

The predominate attraction for migrants to the United States today, is not to work and contribute individual ingenuity to the betterment of the people and the Nation, but rather, migrants are attracted to our poverty. They come because the poor among us have a higher standard of living than the "working class" of most other nations. Why work elsewhere when you can live off the rich in America, who are robbed of their wealth by the Federal Government for redistribution to the poor?

Our political aristocracy allows the rich to hold on to that portion of their own wealth that the politicians deem will appease the rich and continue to ensure political contributions in the future. And with the wealth they extract from the rich, they grant unto themselves and their favored campaign supporters such amounts as will ensure them (politicians) their continued positions of Royalty. With the rest, the professional politicians entrap our poor in an endless, generational cycle of stagnation.

Still, the politicians purchase the votes of our poor with a standard of living that rivals the working-class of most other nations. Our poor have roofs over their heads; furniture in every room; flat panel TV's; cellular telephones; and many have automobiles as well. And with these bounties and the continual promises of even more, our professional politicians buy their way into Royalty and bribe their way into lives of celebrity.

And: what of our precious "middle class?" They were pressed from single bread winner households in the 1950's to dual income homes in the 1970's. In the 1990's they became multi-generational homes, with mom and dad, grandma and grandpa, and their children into the ages of their 20's and 30's and 40's – all pooling their resources to maintain their "middle-class" standards of living.

Patriots love and defend their country, but they wonder how it came to this, and how to restore it. The fruits of the 16th Amendment have proven it to be a bad tree, with roots springing forth from evil and branches stretching outward toward total domination over the lives, the liberties, and the pursuits of every American citizen.

Unless the 16th Amendment is repealed or amended it will continue to grow, like the cancer that it is, until it has fully devoured the wealth of our nation and has suffocated our Constitution – leaving it (our Constitution) and the final remnants of the liberty it protects, dead and utterly vacant of authority and power and promise.

Patriots must rise up and tear down the arrogance of Washington D.C., and evict the self-proclaimed Royalty that now populates the people's Capital, the people's Halls and Chambers and Houses. We must vote the professional politicians out of "our" offices of authority and vote into those offices Citizen Politicians willing to restore America to her proud and faithful Heritage.

To get a king or a prince to diminish the power he has accumulated is like asking an addict to part with his last measure of heroin: he would sooner sell his soul to the death and destruction of those he loves most dear. Likewise, though there may be some patriots in Washington, the majority of our federal politicians will not willingly relinquish their power by returning it to "we the people."

Patriots must stand in defiance of Royalty, and must, with loud and clear voices demand the eviction of the professional politicians: and, must vote in unity for the installment of citizen politicians who vow to restore the Constitution and the liberty of its people.

Excerpt Three from the Constitution of the United States of America
September 17th of 1787, Article 1, Section 4

"The Congress shall assemble at least once in every year."

And dare I suggest it, once is enough! I suspect, though I have no evidence one way or the other, that this Section was included in the inking of the Constitution because in the days of freedom, America's citizen politicians preferred to be anywhere in preference to the Halls of the Federal Government. They had much better uses for their time. They were farmers and inventors and entrepreneurs; they were doctors and educators and pastors; they were anything but professional politicians. They had lives to get to; they had liberty to enjoy; and they had happiness to pursue – none of which was best served by meeting with other politicians so they could pass new laws to inflict upon the people (themselves and their neighbors).

The problem today is that our politicians love passing new laws, because through new laws they increase their power and Royalty: the Halls of the Federal Government have become their own, private candy store. Pass a few laws, ream a few million citizens, and go home richer and more powerful. What a life. Go back next week and do it all again: getting a life-time of pay and benefits and Royal prestige as the comical reward for raping our Nation and eating out the substance of our people.

Excerpt Four from the Constitution of the United States of America September 17th of 1787, Article 1, Section 8

"The Congress shall have Power To lay and collect Taxes, Duties, Imposts and Excises, to pay the Debts and provide for the common Defence and general Welfare of the United States; but all Duties, Imposts and Excises shall be uniform throughout the United States;

To borrow Money on the credit of the United States;

To regulate Commerce with foreign Nations, and among the several States, and with the Indian Tribes;

To establish an uniform Rule of Naturalization, and uniform Laws on the subject of Bankruptcies throughout the United States;

To coin Money, regulate the Value thereof, and of foreign Coin, and fix the Standard of Weights and Measures;

To provide for the Punishment of counterfeiting the Securities and current Coin of the United States;

To establish Post Offices and post Roads;

To promote the Progress of Science and useful Arts, by securing for limited Times to Authors and Inventors the exclusive Right to their respective Writings and Discoveries;

To constitute Tribunals inferior to the supreme Court;

To define and punish Piracies and Felonies committed on the high Seas, and Offences against the Law of Nations;

To declare War, grant Letters of Marque and Reprisal, and make Rules concerning Captures on Land and Water;

To raise and support Armies, but no Appropriation of Money to that Use shall be for a longer Term than two Years;

To provide and maintain a Navy;

To make Rules for the Government and Regulation of the land and naval Forces;

To provide for calling forth the Militia to execute the Laws of the Union, suppress Insurrections and repel Invasions;

To provide for organizing, arming, and disciplining, the Militia, and for governing such Part of them as may be employed in the Service of the United States, reserving to the States respectively, the Appointment of the Officers, and the Authority of training the Militia according to the discipline prescribed by Congress;

To exercise exclusive Legislation in all Cases whatsoever, over such District (not exceeding ten Miles square) as may, by Cession of particular States, and the Acceptance of Congress, become the Seat of the Government of the United States, and to exercise like Authority over all Places purchased by the Consent of the Legislature of the State in which the Same shall be, for the Erection of Forts, Magazines, Arsenals, dock-Yards, and other needful Buildings;--And

To make all Laws which shall be necessary and proper for carrying into Execution the foregoing Powers, and all other Powers vested by this Constitution in the Government of the United States, or in any Department or Officer thereof."

This section of the Constitution details express powers and authorities and duties of the Federal Government. Suffice it to note here that the overwhelming majority of time spent by the professional politicians of Washington D.C. is not spent performing the duties expressed in Section 8 of Article 1 of the Constitution. Rather, our elected officials appear to spend the majority of their time occupied with furthering their own Royal careers and enacting laws in complete violation of the Constitution they are sworn to uphold and defend.

The patriot is frustrated by the political demonetization of the law enforcement agencies and military soldiers who serve our Great Nation with distinction and in fulfillment of this Section of the Constitution. The sacrifices and contributions of our soldiers and protectors are known to us. Your lonely vigil on the wall, along the fence, and in the dark places of the globe is known to us. The debt we owe can never be rightly settled, but know this, you are in our every prayer and in every tear of our pride and gratitude.

Excerpt Five from the Constitution of the United States of America September 17th of 1787, Article 2, Section 1

"Before he (the President) enter on the Execution of his office, he shall take the following Oath of Affirmation: – "I do solemnly swear (or affirm) that I will faithfully execute the Office of the President of the United States, and will to the best of my Ability, preserve, protect and defend the Constitution of the United States."

Excerpt Six from the Constitution of the United States of America September 17th of 1787, Article 3, Section 3

"Treason against the United States, shall consist only in levying War against them, or in adhering to their Enemies, giving them Aid and Comfort."

Is it an aid and comfort to our enemies to inform them of the methods by which we extract intelligence from enemy combatants held within our custody?

Excerpt Seven from the Constitution of the United States of America
September 17th of 1787, Article 4, Section 4

"The United States shall guarantee to every State in this Union a Republican Form of Government, and shall protect each of them against Invasion; and on Application of the Legislature, or of the Executive (when the Legislature cannot be convened), against domestic Violence."

A "Republican Form of Government" is a form of government controlled by the citizens or their chosen (State) representatives. Section 4 of Article 4 of the Constitution of the United States limits the role of our Federal Government with respect to its involvement in State governance. Said more plainly, it is an express role of the Federal Government to "guarantee" (to protect and defend) each State's sovereign rights. And, the Federal Government is to police borders and protect States against invasion. The Federal Government is expressly barred from police actions within State borders, unless specifically requested by State authorities.

If you are familiar with the IRS, then you are as aware as the patriot that the Federal Government regularly breaches this Section of the Constitution. And the IRS is only one of many Federal Policing Powers that violates this Constitutional Protection. And, Policing Powers are not the only rights, powers and authorities held by a "Republican Form of Government." All laws and regulations not expressly granted to the Federal Government by the Constitution of the United States are to be enacted and enforced by citizens and/or their respective State Legislatures.

The Federal "No Child Left Behind" program comes to mind. Educating the populous may be a fine and wonderful thing, but it is not in the Charter of the United States and it is not in the prevue of its Federal

Officials. In a free country, you and your neighbors get to decide how important formal education is – not the Federal Government. Federal politicians can go ahead and cry all day long about how Chinese youth are better at math, and how German youth are better at science, and how British youth are better at English. To which the patriot should respond:

"How delightful: American youth are born free. And we free citizens will see to our own education. Thank you very much for your observations. Now go back to Washington D.C. and beef-up the patrols on my border – you allowed another million invaders to cross last year. By the way, how good are the Chinese and German and British governments at keeping invaders out of their countries?"

Here are some patriotic thoughts on the subject of education:

1. How about we require each student in America to read the Declaration of Independence every year of High School? Maybe they can write reports discussing its meanings to citizens today.

2. How about we require each student in America to read the Constitution of the United States every year of High School? Perhaps they can write reports discussing its meanings as well.

3. How about we stop teaching diversity and start teaching unity? Instead of making our children hate one another for how they are different; maybe we can help them love one another for how they are the same.

4. How about we start teaching English to our immigrant brothers and sisters, so they can prosper together with us? Rather than secure poverty for them by enabling their reliance on languages not common to us all.

5. And why not teach that while our differences make us beautiful and rich and full, it is our similarities that make us strong and free and prosperous?

Regardless what you would have taught in your schools, the patriot would see federal politicians stay in Washington D.C. and take all their swarms of officers with them. Quite frankly, they can count themselves among the invaders we would like to see prevented from crossing our State borders.

Before moving on to the National Anthem, let me share these final thoughts about our Constitution:

I have heard the Constitution referred to as a "living, breathing document" so many times, by politicians who should have their mouths washed out with soap, that I am quite nearly hostile.

What the patriot understands is: "That which lives can die, and, that which breaths can suffocate."

The vary words they (professional politicians) exhale is poison to my ears and death to my hopes for a newly freed and liberated American citizenry. These so-called political leaders, with their every action and their every passed Bill, are killing the Constitution and are smothering its precepts and promises.

How long will we American patriots endure the blatant mass suicide that is the path our political leaders have set before us?

Our beloved Constitution bleeds at every pore and we look dumbfounded at what we allow our politicians to do with our authority. The soul of our dearest patriotic document gasps for its every breath, under the weight of tyranny by our own elected officials, and we stand dismayed at what we have done and allowed to be done in our name.

American Patriotism is about knowing and understanding which governing powers and authorities and rights belong to the Federal Government; and which belong to the respective State Governments; and which belong to the citizens in their local communities. And American patriotism is about one other thing, it is about fighting to protect those powers and authorities and rights; and insuring that they are properly defended in strict accordance with the dictates of our Constitution. Knowing and understanding reflects our patriotic love; fighting and protecting reflects our patriotic devotion.

The Star Spangled Banner
First Verse, 1814, Francis Scott Key

"O say, can you see, by the dawn's early light, What so proudly we hail'd at the twilights last gleaming? Whose broad stripes and bright stars, thro' the perilous fight, O'er the ramparts we watch'd were so gallantly streaming? And the rockets' red glare, the bombs bursting in air, Gave proof thro' the night that our flag was still there. O say, does that star-spangled banner yet wave, O'er the land of the free and the home of the brave?"

Our troops are still brave and do valiantly stand and fight on whatever ground they are commanded to take and hold for our protection and for the protection of our Nation. But can we claim that we are so brave?

Do we march on the Halls of Government and demand they return our Constitutional freedoms? Do we vote for leaders who would restore our hope in Government? Do we place ourselves on the front line of elections: contributing of our time and talents and resources in support of patriotic citizen candidates? Do we vote for what is right, or do we vote for what politicians will give us from the great coffers of Congress?

Our brave soldiers are asked to hold weapons of war and stand hazardous posts in protecting us from foreign enemies. We are asked to protect the Halls of Government from domestic enemies, by demonstrating equal courage and by voting into office those who will not betray our liberty and who will not disgrace our gallant soldiers.

If you want a simple test for detecting a professional politician, ask the candidate what profession he or she was in eight years ago – if the answer is holding a political office, there is a really good chance you are looking at a professional politician. Arrogance is another good test, if a candidate believes he or she is the only citizen for the job, you are probably looking at a candidate with an agenda of Royalty in the making. Citizen candidates have lives and careers outside of politics. They view political participation as a civic and patriotic duty, not as a way of life or as the means to an end.

The Pledge of Allegiance

1892, Francis Bellamy, abridged

"I pledge allegiance to the flag of the United States of America, and to the Republic for which it stands: one Nation under God, indivisible, With Liberty and Justice for all."

When did you last pledge your allegiance to the Republic for which our flag stands? The patriot knows that the "Democracy" of today is more similar to the socialism of some European countries, than it resembles the Republic referred to in our Pledge of Allegiance. But this does not stop the patriot from honoring the flag or pledging allegiance; it simply causes the patriot to have deeper convictions and more stirring emotions as our flag is held high or instead, is disgraced. We patriots love our flag and our anthem as truly as we love our Constitution and our Declaration of Independence. These are the symbols and words and lyrics of our devotion, they are part of what we have in common and part of what unites us.

But if you think you still live in one Nation under God, that is indivisible and which provides Liberty and Justice for all, I ask you to consider these few thoughts:

Is a person living in Liberty who fears the Government Tax Collector more than he or she fears the Grim Reaper?

Is a person living in a Nation of Justice for all, who sees known murderers walking the streets; known thieves living in mansions; and known liars lining the Halls of Government?

Is a person living in an indivisible Nation, who sees citizens divided by race; creed; color; religious beliefs; sexual preferences; income levels; political affiliations; gun rights; and so on?

I ask you, is a person living in one Nation under God, who can speak about the evils of religion while in the Halls of Government, but can not speak about the evils of Government while in the Halls of religion?

We American patriots must do more than shed tears of honor on behalf of our flag and our Republic: we must shed sweat as well – we must work to restore the pride and dignity and promise of our Nation of free citizens.

The Oath of Allegiance for Naturalized Citizens

"I hereby declare, on oath, that I absolutely and entirely renounce and abjure all allegiance and fidelity to any foreign prince, potentate, state, or sovereignty of whom or which I have heretofore been a subject or citizen; that I will support and defend the Constitution and laws of the Unites States of America against all enemies, foreign and domestic; that I will bear true faith and allegiance to the same; that I will bear arms on behalf of the United States when required by the law; that I will perform noncombatant service in the Armed Forces of the United States when required by the law; that I will perform work of national importance under civilian direction when required by the law; and that I take this obligation freely without any mental reservation or purpose of evasion; so help me God."

The Bill of Rights

The Bill of Rights consists of the first ten Amendments to the Constitution of the United States of America. These ten Amendments were introduced in March of 1789, during a Congressional session held in the City of New York. The Bill of Rights was ratified in its entirety on December 15th of 1791.

The express purpose for adding The Bill of Rights as amending the Constitution is contained in its Preamble, stating in part:

"In order to prevent misconstruction or abuse of its (the Federal Government's) powers, further declaratory and restrictive clauses should be added."

The Constitution was ratified on November 17th of 1787, and less than two years later the drafters of the Constitution were already concerned about the Federal Government taking upon itself too much power and authority from "we the people."

In 1791, four years after the ratification of the Constitution, The Bill of Rights was ratified to rein-in and prevent the Federal Government from abusing its role of protecting the rights of the several States and of the people.

First Amendment
December 15th of 1791

"Congress shall make no law respecting an establishment of religion, or prohibiting the free exercise thereof ..."

Because many immigrants to the United States and the former Colonies had fled to America specifically to avoid religious persecution, the citizens wished to insure that their freedom to worship or to not worship in whatever fashion they so chose, would not be obstructed by the Government.

Directly connected to this right to worship or to not worship, was the right to speak freely and without restriction about religious matters, political matters, science and etcetera, without interference by the Government. As such, the First Amendment continues:

"or abridging the freedom of speech ..."

As it stands today, this right of the people has been comparatively well preserved. The Government has abridged religious speech by threat of IRS taxation for speaking about political issues from the pulpit, though they have been good enough to limit these abridgements to the banning of mostly "conservative" political views. For that, I suppose we should be grateful.

Still, you may be less than comforted to learn that our beloved federal politicians are always on the look for new and creative ways to use the IRS and other policing authorities to silence the voices they do not like. Talk radio and "Right Wing" fringe groups are among the early targets on their lists. But worry not, they will eventually find a way to protect you from every voice they do not want you to hear.

I wonder how long it will be before this book is burned at the stake and banned from every library, book store, on-line bookseller, and my own website.

Ultimately, your freedom of speech is only as safe as the freedom of speech of those with whom you most disagree. So, if you think I have patriotism all wrong, and the Government finds a way to shut-me-up, you can be most assured that not far behind me will be the other voices like mine – and those exactly the opposite.

The Government of the 21st century will make drones of us all: allowing us no opinions except those they dictate to us.

Immediately following the freedom of speech clause of the First Amendment, is this:

"or of the press …"

In other words, the Government is not to abridge the free press: the right of the people to establish and print what manner of material they, themselves, deem print worthy. This clause is most often discussed with regard to reporters of the news, but it is not limited to such.

With few exceptions, the Federal Government and the courts have been fairly even-handed with the protection of this right of the people. However, if Congress pushes for greater regulation of the radio air ways, they will have stepped beyond the threshold of this protected right: just as surely as if they pushed for greater regulation of television, newspapers, the internet, or any other source of news or entertainment.

The next protected right of the First Amendment is:

"or the right of the people peaceably to assemble ..."

What could be a more pure indicator of a free nation and a free people? As pertaining to equality under law or equal rights with respect to assembly and association, it is not the place of Government to dictate to the people with whom the people may or may not assemble. If the assembly is peaceable, it is protected – regardless the nature of the assembly or the duration thereof. Liberty and equality means that we are free to choose what we will do; what we will think; what we will say; what we will believe; and with whom we will do these things.

When the Government can say that the Boy Scouts must allow girls into their ranks, the Government suppresses freedom, violates the Constitution, and diminishes liberty and equality.

The First Amendment says we are equal in our rights to peaceably assemble. This is supposed to mean that you are free to choose not only with whom you will associate, but also, that you are free to base that association upon any grounds of commonality that strikes your interest. And if your grounds for assembly do not please me or do otherwise strike me as offensive, I am free to not assemble with you.

Quite frankly, you are probably no more interested in what I find offensive than I am in what you find offensive. But as patriots, we must stand together to protect one another's rights to assemble for whatever offensive and peaceable reasons we each may choose.

I can not stress enough this critical aspect of patriotism: patriotism in America means allegiance to equal liberty above all else – it means that we must be willing to vote for and defend and fight for the rights of others to believe and say and do that which we find most offensive. If you are unwilling to do this, you are a patriot to something other than the Constitution and the America that we claim to love – just as surely as most of our elected officials are patriots only to their own power and Royalty.

This is not something you can have both ways. You can not say on the one hand that you wish to be free to think and say and do what you believe, but on the other hand, you wish to deny this same right to others because you are offended by their beliefs and behaviors.

This is the vary principle the professional politicians have reversed to bring America to her knees: they play us against each other on the basis of our differing beliefs and behaviors.

Second Amendment
December 15th of 1791

"A well regulated Militia, being necessary to the security of a Free State, the right of the people to keep and bear Arms, shall not be infringed."

While the Federal Government's infringement upon the various rights protected by the First Amendment may be arguable among reasonable persons, the assault of the Government upon the rights of "we the people" to keep and bear Arms is not arguable. You may argue regarding the extent to which the Government has infringed this right, you may even debate the correctness or worthiness of such infringement, but no reasonable person can claim that a citizen's right to keep and bear Arms has not been infringed. This is one Amendment to the Constitution that federal politicians have completely thrown out the window along with the proverbial bath water.

When was the last time you slung-on your six-shooter and meandered down Main Street? No you didn't! If you can get your hands on a carry permit, you might be able to sling-it-on in your living room – but just try going outside with it strapped to your hip and you'll be able to clock with a stop watch how long it takes for the long arm of Congress to snap you in shackles: that my dear brothers and sisters is "infringement."

It is not my purpose here to extol the virtues of one gun rights view over another; rather, it is my purpose to simply bring your attention to this: your Federal Government has removed your Constitutional rights without amending your Constitution!

ARE … YOU … LISTENING?

You do not have to own a gun to be a patriot – many do not. You can even believe that people should not be permitted to keep and bear Arms and still be a patriot – many do. But you can not be a patriot and accept that it is okay for the Government to enact laws in violation of the Constitution, without first amending the Constitution!

In fact, the more you hate guns the more you should fight against the Government banning guns without first amending the Constitution. Not because it will be harder to reverse the gun banning law, but because any violation of the Constitution weakens it. The Country that you love is protected by the Constitution. When you allow it to be weakened, you diminish the sovereignty of our Nation. Most nations do not fall by foreign force of arms: they collapse from within. With each weakening of our Constitution, we come closer to our own self-destruction.

Remember, because this is important: the American patriot fights for the rights of people to do those things the patriot finds most offensive. I want to be very clear on this point – I am speaking now about National rights: not State rights; or County rights; or Town rights; or Individual rights. It is entirely acceptable for the American patriot to fight for the Constitutional right to keep and bear Arms today – and tomorrow stand at the City Counsel to fight for a city ordinance banning guns from all public places, or requiring a permit to purchase or carry a gun within city limits.

The patriot recognizes that there is a distinct and unequivocal separation of policing authorities within the United States. And the Patriot relies upon the Constitution and its various Amendments to sort out the dividing lines.

The Constitution tells us that the Federal Government does not have the right to restrict gun ownership. That is the patriot's dividing line. If you live in a State where the State Constitution similarly protects this right, then that is the next dividing line. The next line is County authority, then your City or Town or Hamlet. Finally, there are those rights which are governed within each household and by each individual person.

The entire foundation of Liberty and Freedom (and American patriotism) is based upon this principle: that all rights and powers and authorities are held by individual citizens. That we are endowed with these rights by our "Creator" – whom ever or whatever you believe that Creator to be. That "we, the people" grant unto the various forms of government portions of our power and authority, to provide for the common good and safety and welfare of us all. And finally, that the further removed from our individual homes a government body is, the less power and authority it should have – lest that government body accumulate to itself power sufficient to become abusive.

I am not suggesting that gun laws are the only laws enacted by Congress in violation of the Constitution – in fact, that is my point! Patriots understand that when politicians sign into law regulations that violate Constitutional authority, and we the people do nothing, we give them permission to subjugate us by all manner of tyrannical suppression. And we have!

You let them take your neighbor's guns, because you don't like guns. So, your neighbor lets them stop your preacher from talking about politics from the pulpit, because your neighbor disagrees with your preacher's politics. At the end of the day, you find yourself in a country where only terrorists and criminals have guns, and only fanatical religions talk about politics during religious meetings and ceremonies.

Our professional politicians have us so twisted in knots that we can no longer see straight. If you do not wake up and understand that what the Founders of this Nation had in common has been taken from us, by the politicians who serve only themselves and each other: you and I and our children are destined to live out our lives in a Nation all together lost and foreign to that Nation of promise, for which so many fallen patriots sacrificed their all.

Every man and woman of uniform who has fought and bled to protect your freedom is deserving of your patriotic courage and your faithful devotion to the Constitution.

Ninth Amendment
December 15th of 1791

"The enumeration in the Constitution, of certain rights, shall not be construed to deny or disparage others retained by the people."

Tenth Amendment
December 15th of 1791

"The powers not delegated to the United States by the Constitution, nor prohibited by it to the States, are reserved to the States respectively, or to the people."

Concluding where they had commenced, the drafters of The Bill of Rights captured in the Ninth and Tenth Amendments the collective concern of "we the people" and of the Respective States, that the Federal Government not extend its reach into the lives and activities of its citizenry: to the detriment of our individual pursuits of happiness.

That which is all too clear to the patriot and which can not be too boldly or adamantly extolled is: The Federal Government of the 21st century is not the Federal Government of the Constitution of the United States of America. The three branches (Executive, Legislative, and Judicial) of the Government as presently populated is as the ancient King of England – we have finally completed the 230 year trade of one tyrant across the sea for a thousand tyrants in Washington D.C.

Thirteenth Amendment

Ratified December 6th of 1865: abolished the practice of slavery and involuntary servitude within the United States.

Fourteenth Amendment

Ratified July 9th of 1868: extended the rights of citizenship to all persons born or naturalized in the United States.

Fifteenth Amendment

Ratified February 3rd of 1870: extended voting rights to all male citizens, 21 years of age or older, regardless of race, color, or previous condition of servitude.

Sixteenth Amendment

Ratified February 3rd of 1913: previously quoted and discussed, this Amendment transferred to Congress the power to extract the full measure of dominion over the States, over the people, and over all activities of life, liberty, and the pursuit of happiness.

Nineteenth Amendment

Ratified August 18th of 1920: extended voting rights to women.

Twenty Fourth Amendment

Ratified January 23rd of 1964: extended voting rights to non-taxpayers.

Twenty Sixth Amendment

Ratified July 1st of 1971: extended voting rights to citizens 18 years of age and older.

Key Terms and Concepts

To facilitate meaningful communication and consistent understandings among persons of differing backgrounds and life experiences, it is prudent to establish a common vocabulary. Additionally, it has probably not passed your attention that within the pages of this book are several phrases and terms not otherwise common to traditional political rhetoric. As such, the following discourse is provided to establish such a common vocabulary as may be useful for future conversations and collective understanding.

Conservatives

There are two basic kinds of Conservatives: (1) Fiscal Conservatives, and (2) Social Conservatives. These two kinds of conservatives generally run together politically; and, you can find them in most of the political parties of our time. Fiscal Conservatives believe that the Federal Government should restrict taxation and spending to those activities specifically outlined in the Constitution. Social Conservatives believe that the Federal Government should restrict individual and social conduct to those behaviors consistent with traditional "Judeo-Christian" values.

Conservatives tend to be most comfortable in the Republican Party and have at times dominated the voice and course of Republican Party Politics. Though less ideologically compatible with the Democrat Party; you can find Conservatives within their ranks as well – mostly for reasons relating to family and social traditions. The Libertarian Party is comprised almost exclusively of Fiscal Conservatives.

The general "value system" of Conservatives is very compatible with Constitutional Patriotism. And though Social Conservatives may struggle with some of the more strict applications of "freedom," (particularly freedoms relating to human behavioral preferences) both Fiscal and Social Conservatives tend to have great respect for Life, Liberty and the pursuit of Happiness.

Democrat Politicians

Democrat Politicians say: "Yes We Can"

While the average American may hear Democrat politicians say "Yes We Can," and assume that the "We" refers to the American people, such an assumption would be incorrect. When Democrat politicians say "Yes We Can," they in truth mean, "Yes, We (politicians) Can" – they are talking about what Democrat politicians can do for "The People."

In practice, Democrat Politicians do endeavor (try) to accomplish virtually all of their campaign promises, save one: they continue to fail at enabling bipartisan "change." And why wouldn't they fail to fulfill this promise? The political game as presently constituted always results in the same, predictable outcome: wins for the professional politicians and losses for the rest of us.

Dramatic Course Correction

I have heard it suggested that we need to take small and gradual steps to reclaim our Country and our Constitutional Liberties; after all, they have been taken from us gradually. Personally, this patriot could not disagree more. There is a time for gradual strategies and there is a time for more invasive tactics. Most advanced cancer cases are treated through surgery which is then followed by aggressive chemotherapy. Surgery represents an invasive tactic, while chemotherapy represents the gradual strategy.

It has also been suggested that we should start from the bottom and work our way up the political spectrum: from local elections, to State elections, and then on to National elections. Again, I am at total disagreement. Federal governance is so entwined in State and local governance that correcting our course back to a Constitutional model will require a whole-patient approach.

No, my good and dear friends, this is one serpent that must be slain at the head and cured the whole body over. The informed and enlightened patriot recognizes that we must take (by vote) Washington D.C. first, and then in sweeping reform restore power and authority to State and local jurisdictions.

How many times have we elected patriots to office, well meaning and resolute brothers and sisters of freedom and liberty, only to watch them flounder under the weight of the power and corruption that permeates American politics? They inevitably succumb to the allure of Royalty, or, they barely escape, broken and disheartened by the pressure to compromise.

No, the window of opportunity is narrow and the creature must be taken swiftly and in its whole. With similar unity as demonstrated by the drafters of the Declaration of Independence, we must find leaders willing to lay their reputations and lives in the path of hazard.

Fairness

What does "fair" have to do with anything? Fairness is a device of the weak intellect! Equality and liberty are not about fairness: they never have been and they never will be – as is right and just and true. Equality and liberty are about citizen's rights, they are about access, justice, freedom, and patriotism. Fairness is about being the "same," as if being the same were even possible: which it is not.

Men and women are not the same – and who would want them to be? Blacks and Whites and Hispanics are not the same – no two people are. No race, no gender, and no religion – no identifiable characteristic of the human condition is precisely the same from one person to the next: that, quite frankly, is why we can identify the characteristic.

No, my friends and fellow patriots, fairness belongs on the elementary school playground: not in a reasoned discussion of patriotism, or freedom, or equality, or of the pursuit of happiness in the United States of America.

Liberals

There are two basic characteristics that distinguish Liberals, they tend to be: (1) Fiscally Relative, and (2) Socially Progressive. These two characteristics are typical of all Liberals, though there may be some exceptions. And while you can find Liberals in most political parties, they are overwhelmingly aligned with the Democrat Party – and have dominated Democrat Party Politics for several generations. Fiscal Relativism emphasizes that the Federal Government should tax and spend in accordance with the popular wants of its citizenry, regardless the Constitutional impact. Social Progressiveness demands that the Federal

Government protect all individual conduct and seek social equity, sameness, and fairness: through regulation.

The general "value system" of Liberals tends to run contrary to Constitutional Patriotism. This is not to suggest that one can not be a Liberal and a patriot; what it suggests is that the characteristics of patriotism need redefining in order to accommodate Liberal ideology. Allow me to explain. You will recall that American Patriotism requires love, respect, devotion, and allegiance to the Constitution of the United States of America and to the Country and People it protects. Because Liberal ideology places popular "wants" above Constitutional principles and seeks Governmental participation to "engineer" social change, patriotism for Liberals must be redefined as: love, respect, devotion, and allegiance to Progressive America.

Party Politics

There are hundreds of political parties participating in American politics; and of these only about twenty regularly nominate national candidates. Of the twenty or so most active political parties, six rise to the top:

America's Independent Party

Constitution Party

Democrat Party

Green Party

Libertarian Party

Republican Party

Though, in recent decades, the Libertarian Party has had candidates participate in several Presidential elections, only the Republican's and Democrat's have consistently proven capable of winning the White House and enough seats in the Houses of Congress to direct the course of National Policy.

As so-called "Third Party" candidates, such as those nominated by the Libertarian's, rise to national prominence, their influence typically has the net result of drawing-off votes that would have otherwise been enjoyed by Democrat or Republican candidates. These Third-Party candidates often determine the losers of elections, rather than the winners. Which is to say, which ever Republican or Democratic candidate the Third Party Nominee is most like, is the candidate who will lose the National election – thus handing the victory to the opposing party.

It has often been suggested that a viable Third Party, made up of "Moderate" American voters, would be a refreshing and dynamic improvement to the current "Two Party" system. But this suggestion simply misses the point. The problem with national politics is not that it is a two party system; the problem is that national politics is dominated by professional politicians. Regardless their respective parties, the majority of politicians seek careers of power and notoriety, rather than opportunities to serve the Constitution, the Country, and the People.

There are also debates suggesting that political pragmatism often requires that good people running for public office are compelled to sacrifice their patriotic ideologies in order to get elected. After all, if they don't get elected, what difference do their ideologies make?

The problem with this thinking is two-fold. First, if they do not run on platforms consistent with their actual ideology, then regardless the outcome of the election, the voters and citizens do not benefit from campaign speeches and debates that reveal each candidate's actual beliefs and hopes and plans for the Country. Second, if the candidate is elected, his or her actual beliefs and hopes and plans for the Country will still be silenced: either because they are squashed in the drone of competing ideologies (that were campaigned upon and need to be fulfilled) or, because the candidate in question loses focus and gets caught up in the various temptations that are Washington D.C. – in either case, the net result is the same.

We humans tend to rise to the expectations set for us, even if those expectations are set in the gutter. So, if we do not tell the voters up front what we believe and what they can expect from us – they will expect the same thing from us that they expect from all the other politicians of our generation: they will expect us to lie, to cheat, and to engage in "Royal" favoritism. What this means to the voters who get us elected, and to the other politicians in the "Washington Royalty Club," is that they fully expect to benefit from some of that "favoritism" when it comes our time to divvy it (our favoritism) out.

In terms of party politics, this means that if a party helps get you elected, you can bet they are going to expect you to vote along party lines when Bills come across your desk – even if those Bills run contrary to your "patriotic ideology." And that is how it goes, "we helped get you that seat at the table, and now it's time to pony up." Before you know it, you're voting for pork and earmarks that disgust you, and for laws that expand Government's hold over the States and the people: because that is the way "the game" is played. But never fear they won't hold it against you; besides, in a few months you won't feel the guilt anymore either.

This is why Political Pragmatism is not pragmatic. If you do not gain party support for your patriotic ideology, you are probably seeking support from the "wrong" party. If you do gain party support for your patriotic ideology, when you get to Washington they (other politicians) will know exactly what to expect from you and they will have no grounds to whine when you start doing what you said you would do. Not that this will stop their whining.

The patriot stands for something, and must do so proudly and without compromise. When you are in a battle against evil, every compromise you make gives evil that much more power. And though we might debate about evil, tyranny is much less ambiguous – because we have the Constitution to guide us. And, like evil, tyranny feeds on compromise. Let us consider this principle closer for a moment, because it is a patriotic imperative.

Imagine that you are holding a cooler containing fresh lettuce, tomatoes, and pickles. We have chance to meet at a park and I happen to be holding a paper sack containing bread, ham, and mustard. It occurs to us in that chance meeting that if we combine our ingredients, we can make the perfect ham sandwich.

As we open our respective containers, your cooler and my paper sack, you can not help but notice that my ingredients are far from fresh: my bread is infested with weevils, my ham is moldy, and my mustard is spoiled. Answer honestly, would you rather eat a garden salad made of your own ingredients, or, shall we share that ham sandwich?

Because the answer is so plainly obvious, how about we compromise – we can use my mustard as a dressing on your salad, or better yet, we can make a chef salad using my ham – what say you? Can we find no common ground? How can you be so stuck in your ways?

It is clear that any compromise between your ingredients and mine will result in tainted goods. Your cooler has preserved your contributions, just as the Constitution protects our liberty. Any compromise with evil or tyranny, like the contributions of my spoiled favors, can have but one outcome – the defiling of that which is pure.

There is liberty and there is servitude. Every compromise between liberty and servitude favors servitude. And like mold on a slice of ham, what begins as little spots here and there eventually envelopes the whole of it.

Returning again to the subject of Party Politics, let us expand the conversation just a little more. As for Party Politics, consider that it is not particularly unusual for a politician to switch political parties. Why is this? The answer comes simple when you remember the singular objective of the "professional politician." Politicians switch parties when they believe it will help them win elections. To the professional politician, party affiliation is not particularly critical, having a seat at the Congressional Trough is. Remember, politicians are power addicts, and there is no place on the planet but the Halls of Washington where they can satisfy their appetites.

Some party switchers will claim that their party has moved away from their principles or that they (the politicians) have evolved and are no longer compatible with the party they are abandoning. These statements and others like them are code: they are code for, "I don't believe I will win my next reelection campaign if I remain in my current party."

Career politicians often have high name recognition, and many voters will pull the lever for the name they most recognize. So, switching parties can often turn a sure loss into a fair chance at victory. Personally, if a politician loses an election, I would prefer that the politician go get a real job. It would not hurt Washington D.C. one little bit if our politicians actually knew what it felt like to put in a productive day's work.

But compromise is the nature of Party Politics. When parties and politicians find it expedient, they are more than eager to share the weevil-infested bread – after all, it is the lesser of two-weevils.

Political Parties

Everyone loves a big party, right? Maybe not so right: regardless the original purposes of the political party system, the so-called "two party" system (Democrats and Republicans) that dominates U.S. Politics today is an abomination.

The singular purpose of the party system for voters is to align themselves with likeminded citizens in order to strengthen their respective voices and their common votes. But the "parties" have been high-jacked by self-serving politicians on both sides of the "aisle." While there may be a great diversity of interests and political views among individual citizens, there is no such diversity among the views of most politicians: the overwhelming majority of politicians seek power, and prestige, and Royal treatment.

As a quick aside, the term "aisle" refers to the walkway used by our elected officials to get to their seats in Washington. We Republicans and Democrats may sit together on the bus and in the ballpark, but our politicians in Washington D.C. do not: they are divided by the aisle. And that aisle, in the figurative translation, cuts like a hot iron through the flesh of our Great Nation.

Returning now to our primary topic, allow me to point out that you will not find a discussion of political parties in the Declaration of Independence; in the Constitution; in the Bill of Rights; in the Pledge of Allegiance; or in the National Anthem. This is because United States citizens are supposed to be "united." The problem for us is that united citizens do not serve the designs and purposes of a tyrannical government nor the power craved politicians that populate its Halls and Offices.

I am reminded of the movie "Master and Commander," in which "Lucky" Jack Aubrey, played by Russell Crowe, Captain of the British war ship "HMS Surprise," discusses in humor the idea of choosing between two evils (two weevils). This riddle, as Lucky Jack tells it, is an allegory for the movie and the story it portrays. It is an excellent movie, and for those of us who allow, the story offers lessons for life.

For now, the idea of choosing between two evils is the point. In life, our decisions are often guided by the reality that there may be no good choice, but only a choice among lesser and greater evils. It may be in future elections that citizen patriots will throw their hats in the ring and offer themselves up as candidates for political office. But for now, it seems we must be content to vote for what appear to be the less radical of two professional politicians.

For so long as individual, patriotic, liberty-loving, citizens fail to run for public office, as an apportionment of their patriotic duty, professional politicians, with their silvery tongues and their promises of "gifts o' plenty," will continue to segregate us into parties and pit us one citizen against another.

You may join a party when you register to vote, but you do not have to vote party lines. And as far as it goes, you may have to join a party to have a chance at winning an election to public office, but you do not have to put party politics above patriotism or above your defense of our Constitution: which you are sworn to uphold and protect.

Representative Republic

You have probably noticed that we Americans do not vote for every issue and every proposed law that comes down the pike. Instead, we elect representatives (politicians in the modern speak) to champion and vote on our collective behalf: to settle issues of common concern and to enact and repeal laws as necessary to ensure domestic tranquility. As a general practice, we Americans tend to vote in favor of representatives (politicians) who we believe will best serve our individual interests and fulfill our personal expectations. In contrast, as patriots we vote in favor of representatives who we believe will best serve America and her citizens in accordance with the principles and dictates of our Constitution.

This form of governance (citizens electing representatives) is, contrary to popular myth, not a Democracy, rather, this form of governance is a "Representative Republic" – at times and alternatively referred to as a "Representative Democracy." You can think of it this way: (1) a democracy is a form of government in which citizens have a majority vote; (2) a republic is a sovereign country or state; and (3) a representative is a person elected to represent the people.

Perhaps you begin to see and understand why the two major political parties in America refer to themselves as Democrats and Republicans. And though these party names have long histories, the patriot sees the modern Democrat Party as the popular vote party, and sees the modern Republican Party as the sovereign country party: neither of which is doing a particularly good job at representing the people.

Here is a pop-quiz for you, how many "Republics" are there in the United States of America? You should recognize this as a "trick question," and it should probably offend you just a little that such a question is tricky. There is one reason and one reason alone that this question is tricky, and the reason is that we, in America, are no longer taught "proper" American history and "proper" political science.

To avoid misunderstanding and to provide you with a few moments to consider the question of how many Republics there are in the United States of America, allow me to digress into a brief illustration about the teaching of American history and political science in America today. I am looking now at a book published in 1987 by the U.S. Department of Justice entitled "United States History – 1600-1987." This book was produced for the Immigration and Naturalization Service for distribution to those seeking U.S. citizenship. On page 38 of the text, in a discussion about the differences between the Articles of Confederation and the Constitution of the United States of America, the book explains how the drafters of the Constitution wrote the following language in Paragraph 1 of Article 1, Section 8: "Congress may require states or citizens to pay taxes."

I challenge all readers to justify how the Federal Officials who wrote this history book, given to our immigrant brothers and sisters, could come up with such an offensive interpretation of the Government's Constitutional authority to collect taxes. Before answering this challenge, I invite you to read again "Excerpt Two from the Constitution of the United States of America" as it is presented within "Pure Patriotism," the book you are presently reading.

Returning to the question of how many Republics there are in the United States of America, I offer you the answer with no further delay: there are fifty-two Republics in the United States of America. Let's do the math together, shall we?

Each State is a Republic, and there are 50 States in the United States, which equals an initial count of 50 Republics. According to my assessment, that leaves us with two additional Republics to identify. Have you put names to them yet?

The 51st Republic in the United States of America is the District of Columbia, otherwise and more commonly known as Washington D.C. The District of Columbia, like the 50 States, has both local and federal elected officials, including two Senate Seats and one in the House of Representatives: thus qualifying Washington D.C. as the 51st Republic in the United States.

So, what of our 52nd Republic, have you guessed it yet? Or per chance did you already know? If not, here is a hint for you. We educators love hints, they tend to heighten the cognitive senses and elevate one's consciousness to greater intellectual retention.

When was the last time you Pledged allegiance to the Flag of the United States of America? Together with the Flag, to what else did you pledge your allegiance? Let's walk through it together:

"I pledge allegiance to the flag of the United States of America, (these would be the first 50 Republics previously mentioned) and to the Republic for which it (the flag) stands: One Nation under God, indivisible, With Liberty and Justice for all."

The United States herself is our 52nd Republic. Each citizen of the United States is a citizen of two distinct Representative Republics, and is pledged by allegiance to all 52. You are a citizen of the Republic (State or Washington D.C.) in which you reside, and you are a citizen of the Republic of the United States of America. To memorialize your citizenship, every two years you are invited to cast your ballots (vote) for your preferred State and Federal Representatives.

Historically, respective State Governors and Legislatures have had more impact on and more influence in the lives of American citizens than their Washington D.C. counterparts. But in the generations following the passage of the 16th Amendment in 1913, this historic truth has been laid-to-waste in favor of an ever expanding and intrusive Federal Government – and its leading political officer, the President of the United States of America.

The primary struggle between Republicans and Democrats is a struggle between State's rights and Federal powers; said otherwise, it is the long struggle between the first 51 Republics and the 52nd.

The patriot recognizes that if the Republic of the United States continues on its present course, the remaining 51 Republics will eventually be erased: and with their demise, will follow the last remaining remnants of individual freedom and citizen's rights. The blockbuster movie series "Star Wars" comes to mind. Where do you suppose George Lucas found the plot line for Star Wars? He found it in human history. And lest you think mine are the ramblings of a heretic or a fear monger, I beg you to consider that same world history: because this has been the "too often" repeated destiny of the nations of human kind.

Rome fell to it, and shall we claim that we are greater today than Rome was in its time? Germany fell to it, and shall we claim that we are more pure today than Germany was in the days before Hitler? And the list of nations that have fallen to centralism is as long as human history. Power is given by the people to localized leaders and to a distant central authority. That central authority spreads its influence through ever intrusive edicts until it has subjugated its people and usurped the authority of their local leaders. Then, when the die is cast and the central government has gathered unto itself all the power of the people, a single figure rises forth and mutes the legislature and seizes ultimate authority.

But you think that this could not happen today, not in America, not in a free country. And you would be wrong, desperately wrong. You think this way because the alternative is unthinkable and uncomfortable. Educational instruction today ignores the how's and why's of history, focusing instead on the when's and where's. They have not prepared us for what we are facing today and they have failed to teach us the signs of national self-destruction.

Meanwhile, the politicians of more recent generations have been occupied with gathering their own prestige, and power, and Royalty: caring not for the future corruption they have been and are currently facilitating. The combination of our ignorance and the blind ambition of our political leadership has, indeed and in fact, lead us to that unthinkable and uncomfortable place.

As with so many fallen nations, around the globe and throughout history, fewer than half our citizens take the time to vote, and fewer still care enough to actually study and learn about the content of ballot issues and about the character of political candidates. And contrary to the arguments of our time, the content of character is far more critical to the future of our States and our Nation and our Constitution than so-called "political" experience. Fact is that we do not need leaders with "political experience;" rather, what we need are leaders with "life experience" – leaders of good character who will not sell us out in exchange for personal glory: leaders who will fight for our rights and our Constitution.

Unless you, as an individual patriotic American are willing to stand up and be counted – and are willing to wake up your neighbors to encourage them to do the same, our Nation will very soon and very rapidly lose the Constitutionally mandated protections of STRONG STATE REPUBLICS in favor of a Strong Central Government. And so much power centralized in one body of politicians has but a single, proven course, and that course is national collapse.

Our federal system of government is already corrupt and showing no signs of a desire to self-correct. We Constitutional patriots have less time than we are willing to admit – and this is the actual "inconvenient truth" of our generation. If we do not act immediately, our States will give their final submission to Federal authority within a decade (+/-) thus triggering the final march toward the total loss of our way of Life, Liberty and pursuit of Happiness. Without a dramatic course change, I give us fewer than 25 years before the total collapse of our way of life.

Our greatest hope lay in the prediction itself, because it means that we have time to act – between six and eight years to be precise. The exact period required to replace (by vote) every professional politician in Washington D.C. – because that is what it will take to correct our course. And I am not talking about having patriot politicians occupying a majority in the House and the Senate; I am not even talking about occupying a veto-proof super majority – I am talking about a mega-majority in the House of Representatives, in the Senate, and in the White House.

Our Declaration of Independence was not signed by a majority. Our Constitution was not signed by a majority. And the restoration of our Constitutional Government will not hold for another 200 years on the votes of a majority. To succeed we must pack the Halls and Chambers and Houses of Washington D.C. with an overwhelming citizenry of John Hancock-type patriots – the kind of patriots who are willing to sign their names bold, and clear, and without reservation or concern for the retaliation of "the King."

Before suggesting that we have more time than six or eight years, let me caution you with all my fervor that we do not. Yes, it may take longer than this for the final stroke of our demise, but the opportunity to avoid the calamity will not hold until the twelve o'clock hour.

Our parents and grandparents had more time, and they did little to stem the tide. No, my dear patriot brothers and sisters, we do not have the luxury of time enjoyed by our forbearers. We stand at the precipice, and the final hour for action has fallen to us – we can not pass this hard chore to our children. Not this time. Not our generation. Not because our children could not stomach the fight, and not because it would be cruel to burden them with such a responsibility. No, we must fight this fight and not pass it forward – because if we fail it will be too late.

It is as though we are the last leg of a 440 relay at the State Finals. If we are to continue on to the Nationals and from there to the World Championships, we must finish this race in First Place. Second Place just won't get it done. The baton we hold bares the blood of revolutionaries, the tears of civil war survivors, and the sweat of every patriot who has worked and fought to preserve our Great Nation and its State Republics. If we fail them now, in this final conflict of the Constitution, this final 110 yards of the race, all their blood, sweat, and tears will be preserved only in history: and not in the lives of our children and grandchildren. If you consider me to be waxing melodramatic, please consider these newsworthy realities:

1. The world has decided that the Holocaust of the Second World War (during which millions of Jews and Black ethnic minorities were slaughtered) did not actually occur – soon, like the stories of the Old Testament of the Bible, faith will be required in order to believe in the

Holocaust. The last Holocaust victim has not yet perished, and already they are forgotten to history.

2. The United States Government now owns several banks and manufacturing companies – try finding authority for that in our Constitution. And they did not nibble away at the edges; they went straight to the top, seizing the largest banks and largest manufacturing companies in the United States. I can not speak more plain than this: our Government has no business in business.

3. Federal Officials are playing Charades with science, acting out and acting upon only that science which fits nicely with their political theories and objectives – and ignoring all science that does not lead to political expedience and victory.

4. Federal Officials are now openly mandating State compliance with Federal guidelines, which guidelines are dictated by political groups and individuals operating entirely outside the confines and restrictions of the Constitution.

5. Federal Officials now regularly enact and enforce edicts on local schools; local churches; local charitable groups; local clubs; local law enforcement agents; local housing authorities; local emergency response units; and the list goes on.

You might be interested to know that I wrote this book in April of 2009, but I assure you that this brief sampling of "realities" is not an attempt at April Fools humor.

I am reminded of two riddles:

How do you eat an elephant?

Answer: One bite at a time, of course.

And how do you boil a frog alive?

Answer: The frog will not jump out of the pot, if you put it in when the water is cool and then gradually increase the temperature to a boil.

You are perfectly within your rights to think that I am being melodramatic; just as I am perfectly within my rights to wonder why you have so little concern about your liberty being stolen from you – one bite and one degree at a time?

Republican Politicians

Republican Politicians Say: "Yes You Can"

This puts Republican politicians one tic closer to Constitutional allegiance than their Democrat counterparts, but there is a disconnect between what Republican politicians say in their political mantra and what they do in the Halls and Chambers of Washington D.C. In fact, aside from being more pro-military and more inclined to cut taxes, there is very little to distinguish Republican politicians from Democrat politicians. Both spend; both earmark; both pork; both engage in partisan posturing; and both view political "service" as a "career."

One hope for patriots may be to recapture the attention of Republican Party leadership and compel them to actually live up to their mantra – and start balloting patriotic citizen politicians who, when elected, will fulfill the promise. Perhaps if the Libertarian and Constitution Parties saw Republican candidates who would place the principles of the Constitution ahead of party politics, they would throw their support behind these candidates and help restore liberty, fiscal restraint, and the Constitution to their rightful places of honor and respect within this greatest of all nations. Such candidates might also attract Independents and Moderates to the polls for Republicans, together with the more "right"-leaning Democrats.

Thoughts in Finale

When watching the movie "Gladiator," the patriot roots for Maximus, because Maximus fights for the Republic against Commodus, who seeks to throw-down the Republic and replace it with a Centralized Monarchy.

When watching the movie "Star Wars," the patriot roots for Luke, Yoda, and Obi-wan Kenobi, because they seek to bring-down the Centralized Monarchy and replace it with a Representative Republic.

When you find yourself in the voting booth or in political conversations, do you fight for our Representative Republics and the Constitution that protects them, or, do you support the professional politicians in their quest to replace our Republics with a Centralized Monarchy?

There is a political storm coming, and it promises to change the substance of our Nation. The question patriots must ask and answer is this: am I ready to stand and work and vote for the salvation of my Constitution or am I going to continue watching from the sidelines as the professional politicians, special interest groups, and fanatical activists rip it to shreds?

Issues of Our Generation

There are many issues of interest and debate circulating through American society, and it is not my intent to discuss them all in the context of patriotism. I invite you to join open conversations on the issues of our generation by visiting my website at (www.clay4usa.org). For now, such issues shall be presented as seem necessary to illustrate the mindset of the patriot. The purpose for discussing these issues is not to suggest how an American patriot should "feel" or "believe" about these issues, but rather, the purpose here is to provide examples of how an American patriot ought to "view" the many issues of our time.

I ask you to reflect a moment on how the Founders addressed the issue of human creation. They chose the agreeable term "Creator" and then insisted the Federal Government stay out of the issue. Today's pure patriots view issues through the same prism: they recognize our equality as citizens and then establish the boundaries of Federal involvement.

Abortion

One of the most controversial and emotionally charged issues of our generation is abortion. There are those who believe life begins at conception, others who believe life begins at birth, and still others who believe life begins somewhere between. And the question of when life begins is only one of many questions hotly contested within the overriding issue of abortion.

For the American patriot, the question of when life begins should not be the first question asked with respect to abortion or any other issue of our time. The first question should be: Who has the authority to decide the issue?

The Constitution discusses two authorities relating to the issue of abortion: one is the authority relating to American citizens, and the other is authority relating to "life." The Constitution is specifically ordained to protect the rights of the "people," which could be more narrowly interpreted as the rights of its "citizens." According to Section One of the 14th Amendment, ratified July 9th of 1868, "All persons born or naturalized in the United States, and subject to the jurisdiction thereof, are citizens of the United States and the State wherein they reside." An unborn child, having by definition and by nature not yet been born, is not a citizen of the United States, and therefore has no promise of Constitutional protection as such.

This brings us to the Constitutional authority relating to "life." It is clear that with respect to Life, Liberty and the pursuit of Happiness, the Constitution was drafted, in particular, to protect these rights as the unalienable rights endowed upon all persons, regardless of citizenry. Thus, it behooves us to return to that hotly contested matter of: when does life begin?

It would be so much easier for all of us if we did not have to address this question and this issue. But there it is – the great debate of the 1960's just won't go away. If this were an issue of human kindness or compassion, the debate would have been long resolved, because the Constitution was not established to compel citizens to be kind and compassionate. What we do know is that the Constitution protects freedom and liberty, and, there is the matter of a "woman's right to choose" – choice being the vary basis of freedom and liberty.

To seriously complicate an already challenging social and legal issue, we have the professional politicians weighing-in, whose primary objective is to stir-up animosity and hate so they can extract an ever increasing measure of power. With politicians benefiting from the continuance of the controversy, we citizens find ourselves in a never ending crossfire of anger, and violence, and tears.

As we approach the question of "when life begins," it is important that we air-out the emotions and drill-down to the bitter pain. So, prepare for some hard words. There are three words that come to mind that best describe what an abortion is. These three words would generally not apply together, which is to say that any given abortion is either one of the following:

An abortion may be a sacrifice. A sacrifice would be the voluntary termination of one life in order to preserve or protect the life or wellbeing of another (or others).

An abortion may be an execution. An execution is the legal termination of one life in order to secure justice or tranquility for another (or for others).

An abortion may be a murder. A murder would be the immoral termination of one life in order to accomplish a purpose contrary to human equality.

In determining if a particular abortion is a sacrifice, an execution, or a murder, we must also consider the three parties impacted by the action: (1) the would-be mother of the unborn child, together with those people most closely associated with her (including the would-be father and the unborn child); (2) local, State, and Federal Governments, in their respective roles of authority; and (3) the community at large, which comprises of both geographic and social elements. Matters of life and death impact us all, because they run like ripples through the traditions and practices of our ever developing society.

The determination of an abortion as being a sacrifice, or an execution, or a murder is the primary battleground of the abortion issue. This determination is also at the heart of the debate over when life begins, because of the specter of murder. While it may be possible to sacrifice or execute a non-living thing, it is entirely impossible to murder a non-living thing.

Under current law, as established by the Supreme Court, most abortions performed today would be classified as executions. This is entirely acceptable to those who view the issue on the basis of "a woman's right to choose," but it is vexing to those who fight for "the right to life."

From my perspective, abortion is not a "right," it is a choice; and birth is not a "right," it is an inheritance. Additionally, I do not view abortion as an issue of right and wrong or of good and evil – rather, it is an issue of: when is abortion right and good, and when is abortion wrong and evil?

But I ask the patriot, who is worthy to judge? I certainly know that I am not, are you? If not us, then who is worthy?

The Declaration of Independence suggests that our unalienable rights are endowed to us by our "Creator." The Constitution says that the power of the Government is granted to it by the "governed," in other words, by the people. We then must let the Government establish when an embryo becomes a "life," thus establishing the legal transition from "sacrifice" and "execution," to "murder." Then, let each would-be mother with such compassionate advisors as may be available to her, together with the comfort of her Creator, make the difficult judgment herself.

For us to demand more or less is to demand the destruction of Liberty and the collapse of our Great Nation. If you would judge today when my abortion is murder, tomorrow I will judge for you by what name you may call your Creator. Liberty comes with a price, and that price is often the willingness to endure that which we believe to be unacceptable.

And make no mistake, when we in our lofty places seek to restrict the offensive conduct of others, we invite an endless course of restrictions that ultimately entrap us all. In the end there will be one faith and one sacrament; there will be one master and one obedience; and at the head of the table will be seated the Federal Government – and his inquisitors will be many and his punishers eager to dispense all manner of correction in his name. In that end, after the politicians have succeeded in restricting every behavior that each citizen finds offensive, you can be certain that liberty and freedom in America will only be enjoyed by the politicians themselves.

If you would have a free Country, you must fight for every freedom, especially those freedoms you find most distasteful.

If you are opposed to abortion for religious reasons and you fear the condemnation of God against a Nation that permits such a practice: may I suggest that God protects free nations where the word of God is welcome. There is both good and evil in the world, and so long as a nation is possessed of some measure of good, its evils may receive the tolerance of God. It is only when evil in a land completely suppresses good that such a land is subject to supreme condemnation.

The religious patriot knows that America must remain free, because only in freedom can God's word spread and only in a free nation can God rightly be worshiped. It is the tragedy of planet earth that the struggle between good and evil is so often manifest. And it is the tragedy of American heritage that every evil known to the world finds its way here; but every good is here as well, and that does give some comfort and some hope and some protection from wrath.

Climate Change

Global Warming, Man Made Climate Change, or any of the other half-dozen names for it, is another of the frequently debated and hotly contested issues of our time. It seems that humans, particularly those living in the United States of America, are causing our planet to get hot around the collar. Or is it that we are causing an ice age. If you really want to hear human arrogance, keep listening to those who say that our reorganization of natural resources is some how going to disrupt the balance of the "natural" warming and cooling cycles of the planet.

My goodness gracious, it is not like we are creating new minerals and elements out of thin air: everything we humans "make" is simply a reformulation of things we find lying around the planet. Even our own bodies and dare I say it the gas expelled from herd animals was already here. We breathe in oxygen and we exhale carbon-dioxide, we dig for coal and burn it into energy and various by products – all of which were here millions of years before we came on the scene. It is arrogance run-amuck to suppose we could spin the world off its axis under the weight of our current technological and scientific activities. A single volcanic event dwarfs our contributions, and last I heard volcanoes have been erupting for quite a long time.

But here is the real point of the matter, and it is unavoidable and undeniable, for so long as our population continues to grow, our need for resources is going to grow right along with it. We can conserve until we are freezing in the winter, frying in the summer, and crawling again on all fours, and it will not put a lasting dent in our consumption. It is as if the

Global Warming crowd forgot how to count on their fingers and toes. If we conserve 10% and our population grows by 2%, consumption will still outstrip conservation in fewer than 5 years.

Have you discovered the irony of their argument?

They say we are supposed to conserve so that we can pass to our children and grandchildren a world as clean and beautiful and abundant as the world we inherited. And their solution to making this possible is to conserve our consumption of the world's natural resources. Sound about right so far?

But here is the problem with that faulty logic. It assumes we are having children and grandchildren – and if we do that our population will grow – and if our population grows, we will consume more resources tomorrow than we consumed yesterday: even if we do conserve. The only logical way to reduce consumption is to prevent population growth. So, who gets to decide which of us will have children and which will not? Personally, I'll place my hopes in good-old human ingenuity and adaptability, thank you just the same.

It does not help their cause very much that their loudest and most prominent spokespeople are among the biggest polluters and largest consumers of natural resources on the planet. Sure, they are happy to ask us to cut back on our standards of living, but there is not a snowballs chance in "Global-Warming-Ville" that they will cut back on theirs. When Al Gore moves into an igloo at the North Pole, I promise to start taking him seriously about his views on Global Climate Change. No really, I will, I promise.

Mr. Gore's movie on Global Warming, "An Inconvenient Truth" should have been titled, "Inconvenient Timing." No sooner does he release his movie and Mother Earth enters, to date, a four year cooling cycle (and still counting). World-wide, we Earthlings are burning more unregulated fossil fuels than at any time in human history, and to get even with us the Earth is cooling its jets. You have to love it. Oh, and by the way, has anyone been brave enough to inform Al that there are more Polar Bears today than there have been at any time in recent history? And do you think he knows that Polar Bears are land animals? Not water, not ice, but land! Who are we humans to go telling Polar Bears where they can fish and where they can swim?

Okay, I'll try to stop picking on the fellow, but honestly, his movie has swept the nations of the world like a new religion. And the number of believers is mounting, many of whom are in prominent positions of power: both here in the States and abroad. His science has been utterly debunked hundreds of times over, and yet he grows in popularity and renown. It is another of the sad tragedies of our generation – we would rather accept the doom and gloom antics of a proven fraud, than cherish and enjoy the true splendors of this incredible planet.

Am I suggesting that we be wasteful? No. Am I suggesting that we not be mindful of our trashing of the land, and air, and seas? No. What I am saying is that we humans are more likely to be the solution to planetary problems, than we are to be the cause. When Mother Nature spills millions of gallons of crude oil into the ocean, she does not clean up the mess– she sits back to see what will become of it. But when we cause an oil spill, we are Johnny-on-the-spot to clean up after ourselves. And why wouldn't we, it is the right and proper thing to do. When a fire burns-out a mountain range, we are there within a season to start planting new saplings; when the tides of misfortune threaten to extinct a race of creatures from the face of the Earth, we set aside ample space to preserve the animal and give its kind another chance at survival; and when we ravage the world with war, we rebuild what was lost and add unto it for good measure and compassion's sake.

No, we patriots are not the cruel destroyers of the planet we are often made out to be. We consider ourselves to have been endowed with great blessings and commensurate responsibilities. We would see the world prosper and be replenished, because in it we have part, and its beauties add unto the quality of our Lives, our Liberty, and our pursuits of Happiness.

English – The National Language

If the story of the Tower of Babble teaches us anything about language, it is that without a common language people will naturally segregate themselves. It is equally true that there are many benefits to people speaking several languages; but social networks and cultures depend upon a common language as the conduit or the medium through which relationships are established and progress is made. While patriots readily welcome newcomers, all hope for those newcomers to integrate into the fabric of our culture and enjoy the blessings of our prosperity rely on those newcomers adopting our National language.

I grew up in a household where English was the primary language, but where Portuguese dominated family gatherings. My step-dad is 100%, pure blood Portuguese, and he had a huge extended family that far outnumbered the Anglo-European side of the family tree. Though English was not their native tongue, to the one, every member of my dad's family spoke both Portuguese and English. They kept their native culture and language alive, but they recognized the connection between their prosperity in America and their ability to commune with America's culture – and language is the bridge that unites.

Unless immigrants come to America to rebuild their native land on our soil, I can not imagine why they would not choose to learn our language and adapt to our culture. No, those who resist English as the National language of America are not the immigrants who sacrifice everything to come to our shores in search of freedom and prosperity.

I rather suspect that the loudest voices calling for multiculturalism and language diversity are those who wish to enslave migrants in poverty and imprison them behind an impenetrable language barrier. In the United States of America, English is the language of freedom, and the language of opportunity, and the language of hope.

There are three specific human rights enumerated in the Declaration of Independence and in the United States Constitution, and of these, two are directly and inextricably linked to the English language: (1) Liberty, and (2) the pursuit of Happiness. Not speaking English limits Liberty through isolation, and not speaking English limits Happiness by limiting access to the promises and opportunities of this Great Country.

I find it ironic that the people who call for language diversity are quite often the same people who cry about the "greening" of our nation. I wonder how many millions of trees are cut down in their prime each year to print forms and manuals and all manner of printed material in such a diverse number of languages. Think too of the extra ink and water and energy expended in the making and printing of those hundred's of millions of additional pages. And look at the opportunity for cultural exchange that is lost by not having our immigrant brothers and sisters attend courses in English as a second language. We could create thousands of new jobs for educators, and engage them in rewarding careers helping to build cultural unity, while simultaneously helping lay foundations of hope and prosperity for newcomers to America.

I have yet to hear a cogent and reasoned argument against English being officially inaugurated as our National Language. Perhaps I am not listening to the right people?

I have heard political leaders calling for mandatory Spanish classes in our high schools. Now there's a good idea – I am often perplexed by politicians, who live in our "land of the free," but who seek to enact laws that so obviously limit our freedom. How about we pass a law that makes it mandatory that local teachers and parents decide what is taught in their schools? Now there is a law I can get excited about. But don't hold your breath; you won't see that law on the books until patriots take back the Halls of government. What, do they think that we local yokels want our children to fail in life?

When my daughters went through high school they chose to learn American Sign Language (ASL) as their second language. Both can read, write, and speak English, and both are fluent and practicing their skills in ASL. Of course this means that half the time my wife and I have no idea what they are talking about, but we are learning to adapt. Their desire to learn ASL also created jobs for teachers, including some who were hearing impaired. The teacher's union benefited, the teachers benefited, the school benefited, and my daughters benefited from the opportunity to "choose" between varieties of second languages.

Making Spanish mandatory would destroy the second language programs of most schools, eliminate thousands of teaching positions across the nation, and ultimately do no favors for our children or for the Spanish speaking population living within our borders. What will help our Spanish speaking brothers and sisters is teaching them English. But I guess that is just too obvious for the politicians in Washington to grasp.

GDP

Our Gross Domestic Product (GDP) refers most generally to the productive economy of the United States of America. Basically, you add up the sales of all goods and services produced in the United States, and that is our GDP. The significance of GDP in a country like the United States, where taxes are levied against the people in order to fund Government activities, is that you want to avoid having the Government place too great a burden against the production of the economy: to do so invites economic stagnation (or worse) and a decline in the average standard of living for our citizenry.

Any given economic system will typically progress through an established sequence of stages. In other words, the sources of a country's GDP can be expected to follow a predictable course. This course or sequence of stages is as follows:

Foraging

Agricultural

Industrial

Technological

Informational

As a nation progresses through these "general" stages of economic development, the bulk of that nation's GDP will be derived from the source indicative of its stage. Naturally, not all of its production will come from a single source, but as a nation progresses through the stages, the focus of governmental attention typically follows the nation's most productive segment.

Think of it this way, when the Mayflower found its way into Cape Cod Bay in November of 1620, they would have typified the Foraging stage of economic production. The settlers would have hunted animals for skins and meat; wood to burn for warmth; and such vegetable life as could be found for sustenance. But as the seasons changed, the planting of crops and husbandry of animals would have commenced and the economy would have begun to shift from Foraging to Agriculture. As time permitted and as the settling-in process took hold, some of their growing populace would have begun to move from Foraging and Agricultural endeavors, into furniture making, and wagon building, and all manner of Industrial activity. In time, as food and shelter production became more stable, more and more of the people would begin inventing and making things to improve the quality of their lives.

Many economies struggle to move from Foraging to Industry, but the settlers of the "New World" were highly motivated and ultimately proven capable of taming and mastering the land: so, Industrialization of the America's was a comparatively rapid transition. Obviously Agricultural activities have never stopped in America, but the proportional number of persons required to maintain our Agricultural Base have diminished as our skills and our population have grown and developed.

Eventually, the ingenuity of free spirited Industrialists would harvest new inventions that either improved efficiencies or bettered the quality of citizen's lives. And this is where the first fruits of Technological advancement came into play. The telegraph, electricity, the cotton gin, and production-line manufacturing are counted as examples of early technological advancement. During the 20th Century, America shifted dramatically from an Industrial economy to a Technological economy. Today, America is mostly about Information. We sell our "ideas" to companies in other nations to be produced; we clog our courthouses with arguments over the meanings of words; and we copyright, patent, and consult our way to prosperity. We have transitioned into an Information-based economy: not exclusively, but quite significantly.

The concern for the patriot specifically and for the American citizen generally is that what typically follows the Information Stage is the Decline Stage – and declines have historically resulted in national collapse. That is correct. Unless we set a positive course for avoiding financial ruin, America is poised to repeat this historic precedent. And our professional politicians in Washington D.C. seem hell-bent on ensuring that we do not miss our chance to complete this final stage of the GDP cycle. Together with their willing brothers-in-arms in the legal system, and their special interest groups country-wide, our politicians are making certain that billions of dollars are spent each year on deciding who has which rights to what. Not producing a flat dime's worth of substance, but careening through our Nation's wealth as though each citizen among us has trillions to burn.

As more GDP is traded each year in exchange for various forms of paper, rather than for hard goods and the labor that goes into the development of those hard goods, we, as a Nation, move ever closer to that predictable fall. It would take a smarter historian than this patriot to identify a single nation or political economic system that has managed to immerge victorious from the Information Stage.

But I can tell you this: the United States is in a prime position to prove that it can be done, because our political system is founded on the precept that all Government authority is derived from its citizenry. This means that if the Government will get out of the way, the ingenuity and hard work efforts of our self-directed citizenry will plow that new territory with eagerness. But if patriots do not regain control of the Halls of Government, the cause will be lost, because those presently entrenched in the seats of Federal power are apathetic (at best) to the economic future of our Nation. Obviously it is much more critical (to politicians) that we measure the gas output of herd animals. What can they possibly be thinking?

If we patriots will muster the courage and conviction to reclaim our powers from the Government and reinstate our Constitutional standard of governance, we have a fighting chance to preserve our way of life beyond the exhaustion of our Information Stage and to regain our position at the top of the "food chain." I for one am a patriot who is unwilling to give up on the dream that is America the Beautiful, the Land of the Free, and the Home of the Brave.

Here is how it would play-out:

In taking back the Halls of Government from the professional politicians, and reinstating the Constitution as the "rule of law" in America, we would set the Nation's ingenuity and industry free to re-start our economy and diversify our sources of GDP. Working together with our Technological wizards, we will set our Foragers and Industrialist loose to explore and excavate our natural resources, (in environmentally conscious ways) and to transport, refine, and engage those resources into GDP we can be proud of and from which, wealth can be garnered.

Simultaneously, we will re-establish our Agricultural superiority. And with the assistance of Industry and Technology, we will create millions of new, high paying jobs expanding our infrastructure of energy, water, and transportation capabilities. It is absolutely a crime that we live in a country that has tens of millions of citizens living in draught, while we watch billions of gallons of fresh water dump into the ocean. And we have high, ever increasing utility rates in a country that has more stored energy than most every other nation of the world combined.

I wonder how loud our enemies laugh and how bitterly our allies cry when they look upon what we allow our politicians to do. If it were not so unforgivable, it would almost be funny: the richest land in all the world starves and impoverishes itself for guilt sake and arrogance.

And what is with letting less capable nations beat us on Technology and Industry? Are we crazy or something? Did I miss the memo? Let's cowboy-up and get our pride back on! I am sick of pompous, professional politicians telling me that I am evil for everything I do from turning on my lights to driving my truck at 65 miles per hour down the freeway. And why am I still calling it a freeway? I now have to pay a toll to drive on it!

How about this, when their (politicians and environmentalists) "carbon footprint" is only twice the size as my own, maybe then I'll take a day off work to listen to their drool – until then, why don't those resource pigs shut up and let me go about my business? Quite frankly, their two-faced, forked-tongued, hypocritical lies and blather irritate me to no end. Most of them wouldn't know a productive day's work if it took a ride with them in their gas guzzling, carbon emitting, chauffeured limousines.

Now don't get me wrong, I think limousines are sweet – I just have a problem with hypocrites. They travel around America telling us we are killing the planet every time we flush our toilets. Then they travel around the world telling anyone who will listen, that America is the cause of all the world's problems. Does that sound to you like the conduct of a patriotic American?

While we are on the subject of getting our pride back on, how about we reclaim our number one positions in the fields of Science, Engineering, and Invention? If Government would get out of the way of our best and our brightest, America would knock their socks off and we would again lead the world in these fields.

In case there was any doubt, I am not afraid to say that I will put human life and happiness above the natural environment every time I am asked. If they were honest about it, the environmentalists would admit the same: I should know – I am one. I don't know a single one of us (environmentalist) who does not live in a house, drive a vehicle, talk on a cellular phone, watch television, or eat processed foods. So, when was it that human life stopped being part of the "natural" world? If we evolved from nature, then we are part of nature, and what we do is natural.

Please do not mistake my diatribe as a declaration that we should purposefully rape the planet of all that makes it beautiful and abundant. Nothing could be further from the truth. We patriots love our "Country," and integral to "our Country" are the land, the rivers, the mountains, the oceans, the deserts, the skies, and all the living things that are within the boundaries of our dominion. But remember, it is our dominion: we exist as the Creations of Mother Earth or of the Supreme Master of the Universe, but in either case, we exist; and our survival is a direct reflection of our ability to master our environment.

Those who claim to place the natural environment above mankind seldom prove it. While in contrast, those of us who place mankind above the natural environment are the better caretakers; because we recognize that our survival and happiness are symbiotic with nature and the natural environment in which we live. Still, our happiness and survival depend upon more than the environment alone – gainful employment and economic viability are equally important to Life, Liberty, and the pursuit of happiness.

Going Green

We patriots do accept that "green and renewable technologies" are important and they must be integrated into our plans for revitalizing our Country and our economy. But we must exercise wisdom and prudence in the transition from static to renewable resources: we must expand all industry and technology together to meet the demands of current and future human needs.

Immigration and Naturalization

Immigration, from an American perspective, refers to people from other countries and nations of the world wanting to migrate to the United States. Immigration does not make a distinction about the reasons why, nor does it address the legality of the migration: the term simply denotes that a person not born on American soil has come to reside on American soil. In contrast, Naturalization refers exclusively to the process by which a person not born on American soil becomes an American citizen: thus transforming a migrant into an immigrant.

For the more recent 30 years, the issue of "legal" and "illegal" immigration has been a hot and controversial political and social topic: primarily with respect to persons from Mexico migrating to the United States. I have no interest in discussing the various arguments of the issue in this text; however, with the heightened anxiety resulting from recent terrorist actions against the United States, it compels me to discuss the matter as it relates to the patriot's perspective.

Number One: it is impossible to conceive how a country (such as the United States) can claim and preserve sovereignty, without first securing its borders and controlling human migration.

Number Two: America was founded by immigrants for the purpose of establishing a land in which immigrants might find refuge. We present-day patriots can argue about immigration all day long and it will ultimately amount to nothing if we lose our heritage in the wake of so much ire. And though "our Lady Liberty" may have been the making of a French artisan, we have adopted her as our own and have made her a cherished symbol of our freedom and our resolve.

Listen once again to her cry to the world: "Keep, ancient lands, your storied pomp! Give me your tired, your poor, Your huddled masses yearning to breathe free, The wretched refuse of your teeming shore. Send these, the homeless, tempest-tossed to me, I lift my lamp beside the golden door!" (from "The New Colossus," by Emma Lazarus 1883 and inscribed upon the pedestal of the Statur of Liberty in 1903)

The patriot does not close the door to such as these, demanding only the rich and the educated to cross our shores. But there is nothing in this long-enduring declaration that says we must welcome criminals and terrorists. No, those escaping fear and tyranny are our welcome brethren, not those bringing it to our "door."

Number Three: the discourse of "amnesty" verses "path to citizenship" needs to end – it is tearing us apart. And while I respect the absolute need for moderating immigration, the idea of "quotas" to immigration is no more palatable than the "quotas" exercised in every other socio-political application of our time. The standards for Naturalization must be based first on National security and then on the standards of the Oath of Naturalization: you will find a copy in this text.

Number Four: this is one issue where the Federal Government is supposed to take the lead. But as with so many other Constitutional responsibilities, our federal politicians see no advantage in resolving it. In other words, maintaining their Royalty is not contingent on performing their Constitutional duties: professional politicians receive greater benefits from hatemongering and from issues involving social re-engineering.

Thus, our politicians waffle to and fro on matters of border security, immigration, and naturalization, so they can keep the social aspects of the issue alive and kicking. Because, in antagonizing social hatred and exciting domestic insurrections among us, the professional politicians gain a bounty of our power. Therefore, it falls to patriots to see the issue of "illegal immigration" for the "red haring" that it is: another in the long list of issues manipulated by our esteemed politicians to keep us forever in need of their blessings.

Property Rights

Property rights in the United States of America are inseparable from liberty and the pursuit of happiness. You can not be free to pursue happiness, if you have no opportunity to "own" the mechanisms (property) of self-sustenance and pleasure. And it is important to note that "property" does not refer exclusively to "land." Property also includes rights and privileges; automobiles; entertainment technologies; access to common utilities; copyrights and patents; investments; appliances; food; and everything else you claim to "own." These are all part of "Property Rights."

The Government has recently decided that if you own property that could generate more tax revenue if it were owned by a different citizen, they have the right to seize your property and give it to that other citizen: all in the spirit of the "common good." Our Government has also devised a mechanism by which it can seize private American companies and turn them over to alternate owners, including owners not of United

States citizenry. Additionally, the Federal Government is now wielding its power – full throttle, and taking control of State bureaucracies.

No reasonable person can defend such practices by the Central Government as having any basis in the Constitution or for the protection of our citizen's rights to life, liberty and the pursuit of happiness. Those who are defending such Government practices are either being paid to do so (such as attorney's) or are doing so only because the Government hasn't yet come for their property. But I caution such detractors, the Government's insatiable hunger will soon bring him to your gates – and when he comes, there will be none left to protect you and your property from his collectors.

Same Sex Marriage

How is this for saying it plain? If you believe that politicians care about same sex marriage, then you are an idiot. What politicians care about is the "issue" of same sex marriage.

Where there is an issue, there is an opportunity. It's kind of like, "never let a good disaster go to waste" – disasters provide opportunities to get away with things that would otherwise be very difficult or impossible to accomplish. The definition of politician should be, "slight-of-hand expert," because politicians are all about distracting you with one thing (issue) to keep your attention away from what they are really after.

In the case of same sex marriage, politicians see it as an issue they can milk for decades to come, just like the issues of abortion and global climate change. They recognize that same sex marriage is an emotional issue with very strong religious undertones. All they have to do is stir the pot from time to time and watch it boil over into the streets of America.

That boiling over is sold as a disaster requiring Government intervention – after all, maintaining domestic tranquility is one of its roles. Never mind that our mighty and benevolent politicians are usually at the source of the boiling – like anyone really cares who hooks-up with whom.

Personally, I have been perplexed by this particular issue from day one. My wife put it to me this way: "the word marriage is just a word." She went on to explain that "it's what goes into a marriage that defines it. And ours must not mean much if it's threatened by what same sex couples do." In contrast to my wife's point, my concern had always been that if we redefine the meaning of marriage, what is next? Besides, in a marriage there is a husband and a wife – this new definition is going to "redefine" much more than a single word, it is going to redefine society.

Most of the concern over redefining marriage is not based on any of these arguments; instead, the contest has become one of competing views on equality – equal rights. The fact of the matter is that we are fighting over equal rights to define a word! And that is where the perplexing part has always rested for me. In all "fairness," words are symbols and symbols have meanings, and those meanings may indeed be worth defending, but at what cost?

In the end, only the politicians are likely to win this one: because it does not matter to the politicians what we think or believe or feel on the issue of same sex marriage, what matters to the politicians is that not everyone thinks and believes and feels the same way. It is in hate and friction that politicians increase in power and fame and Royalty. For them, it is hate that matters – because hate is energized, hate is heated, hate is power! And it is power that they seek.

Besides, if most marriages end in divorce, I can not fully understand why same sex couples are even interested in such "equality."

If we heterosexual couples could find another word to define our civil unions, one that did not so frequently end in the work "divorce," we would be on it like hot cakes – abandoning "marriage" to any and all takers.

So where are we today?

Straight couples want to call their union, marriage.

Gay couples want to call their union, marriage.

Straight couples do not want Gay couples to call their union, marriage.

Gay couples insist that they have equal rights to use the word marriage.

Straight couples claim that tradition is on their side.

Gay couples claim that the law (Constitution) is on their side.

Straight couples say that marriage is between one husband and one wife, and gay couples have either two husbands or two wives – so it just does not work to call it a marriage.

Gay couples say that those are word games played by Straight couples in order to deny them (gay couples) of their legal rights.

Straight couples state: "then we will change the law."

Gay couples state: "then we will go to court."

And the pot runneth over, and the politicians garner more and more power, and we the people fight, fight and fight, and we lose, lose and lose. For all we know, the politicians have planted protesters on both sides of the "issue" just to insure that the pot boils, boils and boils.

Here is the truth of the matter: We have all been distracted – today, this is mostly a State matter, but it will soon become a Federal case. And when Washington D.C. gets hold of it, every citizen in the United States will lose liberty to it: because, while we think the issue of same sex marriage is about defining marriage, politicians rightly recognize that it is an issue about power.

The challenge for patriots is that the issue of same sex marriage is already permeated with hate and animosity on both sides. We have allowed our politicians to convince us that this is a gate-keeper issue, and that for both sides – it is do or die. Gay activists believe winning this issue will lead to more civil rights for homosexuals. Straight activists believe losing this issue will lead to the legalization of extreme deviance, such as bestiality, polygamy, and adult-child relationships.

For the most part, both sides are probably correct. The problem is that it will nearly be a mute point, because by the time we reach those ends: (1) there will be few rights, civil or otherwise, for any of us; and (2) all those "deviant" practices are already occurring in America.

What I fear most is that this issue, more than any other, will be the un-doing of patriotism. Because there are true patriots on both sides of the same sex marriage debate – patriots that are being pitted against one-another by the professional politicians: patriots who, if they do not calm the hate within themselves, will trash life, liberty, and the pursuit of happiness in "moral crusades" that can only result in one ultimate and predictable condition – Constitutional death!

We are either a free Nation or we are not. We either fight for the rights of others with whom we disagree or we sacrifice liberty on the altar of hatred.

If you fight against same sex marriage because God would find it an abomination, I understand your position, in fact I share it. But the question the God-fearing, Christian patriot must ask is: if Christ prevented the stoning of the harlot, how then would He (our Savior) treat the homosexual?

If you fight for same sex marriage because "we the people" have given you that right in the Constitution, I understand your position, in fact I share it. But the question the Gay patriot must ask is: just because I can do a thing, does it necessarily follow that I must or even should do that thing? Besides, if differences and diversity are beautiful, then why not use a different word to define same sex unions?

Every choice we make comes with a price. In the case of patriotism that price is often the reality that in protecting our own freedoms we invariably must protect the freedoms of those with whom we adamantly disagree. And while some believe that we invite the condemnation of God by permitting practices we find abominable before God, at times we imperfect creations must accept that if not for our collective freedoms, we would not be able to practice our religions and we would not be free to believe in the abominations of God. If I am free to believe that homosexuality is an abomination, then others must be free to believe that it is not.

As united patriots caught up in a desperate battle to win back our Country from the professional politicians, what are we to do about same sex marriage?

The same thing we do about everything else! If it is not within the scope of authority given to the Federal Government by the Constitution, we must demand that the Federal Government preserve the rights of individual States and respective citizens – and does not get involved in the

90

matter. We must demand the "peaceable" and "tranquil" resolution of this issue. We must keep the issue at the State level, or better yet, at the County level – as is the case with an ever diminishing number of other social issues (such as the sale of alcoholic beverages).

If you wish to fight for one side or the other on this issue, that is wonderful. But as an American patriot and a true citizen of the Constitution, you must also fight to keep this issue from becoming a Federal case. Do you really want to add the authority to decide who can marry, to the ever expanding list of "powers" that "we the people" have transferred from ourselves to the Central Government?

In the end, the First Amendment to the Constitution of the United States of America declares: "Congress shall make no law … abridging the right of the people peaceably to assemble …"

Though arguably most sacred, marriage between two people is the formation of a union. And like all other unions under law, marriage is protected by the right of assembly with whom ever we so choose, and for so long as we so choose.

Size of Government

We hear an awful lot about the Government getting too big; problem is that "size" is relative. A size 13 shoe sounds pretty big to me, but I might think otherwise if I were a 6'8" Power Forward in the NBA.

Taxpayer groups and "Conservatives" say they want smaller Government, but I don't think that is what they really mean. I think what they really want is a Government that exercises fiscal responsibility and social restraint; at least that is what the pure patriot seeks. What I mean by social restraint is that patriots would like the Government to restrain itself from getting involved in society's social issues. What I mean by fiscal responsibility is that patriots would like the Government to be efficient and productive with the people's revenue. Both of which would be 100% satisfied if we could get the Government to abide by the Constitution.

Thoughts in Finale

The day-to-day activities of American citizens are under assault by professional politicians, special interest groups, and fanatical activists. People who are so committed to singular causes that they are willing to destroy Liberty in order to compel all Americans to live and behave in accordance with their hyper-monistic beliefs and standards.

While we must protect the rights of all Americans to believe; and speak; and peaceably assemble in accordance with their respective and collective desires: we must equally protect each American's rights to live; and behave; and pursue happiness in accordance with each citizens own, individual desires.

The bottom line regarding the patriot's view on the issues of our generation is that we must keep social and economic issues on the State and local level. Allowing federal politicians to involve themselves in our affairs invites them to extract power from us – with which they subjugate us.

Duties and Mantra

It is now time to synthesize what we have discussed into meaningful language that is easy to understand and practical to apply. It is not the intent of this writer to suggest that the following synthesis provides a complete and defining representation of all that patriots must think and say and do to evidence their patriotism; rather, the intent herein is to ignite the restoration of Pure Patriotism by shining light on what patriotism in America once meant, and can once again mean.

Patriotic Duties

What patriots must do is: <u>defend the Constitution</u>. How patriots must do this, is to:

1. <u>Bear Allegiance to All 52 Republics of the United States</u>

- Respect and defend the rights of each Republic to govern in accordance with the powers and authorities granted unto them, by the people, through the Constitution – no more, no less.

- Study ballot issues and candidates; speak up about what you learn; and vote in every election – the idea that we can not talk about religion and politics in social situations was not suggested by nor is it repeated by patriots.

- Participate in the election process by: (1) running for local, State, or Federal public office and if elected, holding such post for no more than one or two terms; (2) volunteer or campaign for other citizen candidates; or (3) participate in voter registration and get out the vote campaigns – there are countless ways to help.

- Discourage the practice of "professional politicians" – if a patriot is compelled to enter politics for more than eight years, let that patriot "serve" in multiple local, State and Federal offices; rather than holding a single post for more than one or two terms.

2. Adamantly Defend the Separation of Powers

- We must trust the separation of powers as delineated within the Constitution, and restrict the Central (Federal) Government from stepping beyond its Constitutionally prescribed powers and authorities – and where it (Central Government) has already exceeded its authority, we must demand its retraction.

- When a question or doubt arises regarding a particular power or authority, such power or authority belongs to the States or to the people, and not to the Central Government.

3. Place National Liberty Above All Other Commitments

- Without National Liberty, our freedoms to believe, and say, and do, and to assemble will continue to erode, until they are utterly extinguished – we must preserve our rights and powers and authorities within our communities, by demanding that the Federal Government NOT get involved in every social and economic debate that rises to anger.

- We must demand that our federal politicians remain in Washington D.C. and leave social and economic problems (challenges) to be resolved in our respective communities, and Counties, and States.

4. <u>Live as Patriots Live</u> (with love, respect, devotion, and allegiance)

- Love is an emotion that incorporates passion, and excitement, and delight – we must ignite within ourselves and inspire within others an undiluted love for our Country, our Constitution, our People, and our Selves.

- Respect is a combination of appreciation, gratitude and honor – which requires an understanding of the history of our Nation and of our forbearers, and which is demonstrated by our conduct, and our contributions, and our acceptance of responsibility for the preservation of our National Traditions.

- Devotion is commitment demonstrated through action – patriotic action includes: voting; serving in the armed forces; serving in political offices; and perhaps most importantly, working to earn a living which contributes to our National GDP and to the betterment of all our pursuits for happiness.

- Allegiance is the aligning of oneself with that which is greater than oneself, and which is demonstrated by a willingness to sacrifice all in its defense – and while we rightfully honor those who make the ultimate sacrifice of blood in defense of our Constitution, our Nation, and our People: those of us who remain and live must carry the difficult burden of sacrificing our time; and our talents; and our sweat; and our complacency; and our apathy; and our laziness on the alter of our allegiance.

One last word on the subject of living life as a patriot and demonstrating our respect for our Constitution, our Nation, our People, and our Traditions: we need to find a way to restore "respectful conduct" to our culture. Here are a few examples of what I think characterize the conduct of a patriot:

We can leave everywhere we go just a little cleaner than we find it: picking up our trash and yes, even the trash of others at our parks, at our beaches, on our sidewalks, and in our many other public places.

We can proudly and respectfully display our "Stars and Stripes" and gratefully acknowledge others as they do the same.

We can help the young and the elderly to safely cross the street; and lift their spirits with good cheer and kindness as they go along their way.

We can remove our "hats" (symbolic for showing respect) to honor our Flag and our Anthem. We can tip our "hats" to soldiers in uniform whenever and wherever we encounter them. Today, these signs of respect may take the form of standing (or sitting) tall, looking them in the eyes, and whispering "thank you" or, even a simple nod with a pleasant smile will convey the message of your appreciation and honor and respect. And do not be afraid to shed a tear or two as you consider the sacrifices their uniforms represent.

We can vote for what is best for our Nation and our Constitution; instead of voting for what we can take from them.

These and many other simple gestures may ultimately prove to be the key to restoring our liberty, or perhaps, when these symbols of respect become popular again, they will be signs of our success.

Patriot's Mantra

Mantra is a word that holds differing meanings: it can be interpreted both positively and negatively, depending upon the speaker and the audience involved. To avoid conflicting interpretations in the context of this dialog on "Patriot's Mantra," let us agree that "mantra" bears the following meaning: "those words and beliefs frequently repeated by patriots that are capable of transforming instinctual desires into focused actions."

One: If it impacts all the people of the United States equally, it is in the Constitution, or should be added to the Constitution by amendment.

Two: If it does not impact all the people of the United States equally, it should be of no interest to the Federal Government.

Three: The Constitution is not about the authority and power of the Federal Government, it is about the authority and power of the people.

Four: The Constitution informs the Federal Government what it must do, so that it will know what it must not do: which is everything else.

Five: We the people of the United States of America must stand together in defense of our Constitution, our Nation, and one-another: regardless our individual beliefs on the issues of the day.

Six: We are united by our language, our borders, our Constitution, and our belief that we are all equally endowed by our Creator with unalienable rights to Life, Liberty, and the pursuit of Happiness. This stands true, regardless our individual beliefs regarding the manner of our creation or the nature of our Creator.

Seven: Balancing the Federal budget is too low a standard; the Government must operate at a surplus, to be carried forward as a reserve against future calamity or to be returned to the citizenry in proportion to their respective contributions.

Eight: Professional politicians are unwelcome in a nation of free people.

Nine: If I am to call myself an American patriot, I must be willing to fight for the rights of others: to say and do things which I may find personally offensive.

Ten: No people can remain free in a country where property can be taken without consent from one citizen and given to another.

Eleven: A government that imposes its' will upon the people, or deliberately enters upon the private property of a citizen, without consent or a just warrant, is by definition: tyrannical.

Twelve: If I am unwilling to stand upright for liberty, I am destined to kneel captive in servitude.

The Beginning ...

Join us at:

www.purepatriotism.com

Clayton Thibodeau is available for book signing and speaking engagements. Detailed information is available at the above website.